BAIXA-CHIADO
ANJOS
MOURARIA-ALFAMA
GRAÇA
MOURARIA
BAIRRO ALTO
CHIADO
BAIXA
Hospital Miguel Bombarda
Hospital de Santa Marta
Hospital de Santo António dos Capuchos
Hospital de São José
Hospital do Desterro
Polícia Judiciária
Jardim Braamkamp Freire
Avenida da Liberdade
Museu Etnológico da Sociedade de Geografia
Coliseu
Palácio Foz
Praça dos Restauradores
Restauradores
Estação Central do Rossio
Miradouro de São Pedro de Alcântara
Igreja de São Roque
Teatro Dona Maria II
Rossio
Praça Dom Pedro IV
Praça da Figueira
Elevador de Santa Justa
Museu Arqueológio do Carmo
Baixa-Chiado
Museu do Chiado
Praça do Município
Ministérios
Praça do Comércio
Ministério
Welcome Center
Cais das Colunas
Castelo de São Jorge
Museu das Artes Decoratives
Santa Luzia
Santo António de Lisboa
Sé (Catedral)
Nossa Senhora Conceição Velha
Mercado do Forno do Tijolo
Miradouro Nossa Senhora do Monte
Convento Nossa Senhora da Graça
Miradouro da Graça
Martim Moniz
Intendente
Anjos
Avenida
Terreiro do Paço
Estação Fluvial Terreiro do Paço
Doca da Marinha
Cais do Sodré
CAIS DO SODRÉ
Gare Fluvial
Elevador da Bica
AVENIDA DA RIBEIRA DAS NAUS
AVENIDA INFANTE DOM HENRIQUE
RUA DA ALFÂNDEGA
RUA DA BETESGA
RUA DA PALMA
RUA DOM PEDRO V
RUA D MISERICÓRDIA
RUA DO ALECRIM
RUA AUREA
RUA DA PRATA
AVENIDA ALMIRANTE
RUA DE DONA ESTEFÂNIA
RUA GOMES FREIRE
RUA DUQUE DE LOULÉ
RUA CONDE DE REDONDO
RUA LUCIANO CORDEIRO
J
K
L

Fodor's

Lisbon's 25Best

by Tim Jepson

Fodor's Travel Publications
New York • Toronto
London • Sydney • Auckland
www.fodors.com

How to Use This Book

KEY TO SYMBOLS

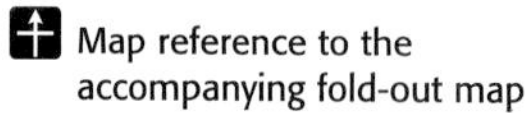

- Map reference to the accompanying fold-out map
- Address
- Telephone number
- Opening/closing times
- Restaurant or café
- Nearest rail station
- Nearest Metro (subway) station
- Nearest bus route
- Nearest riverboat or ferry stop
- Facilities for visitors with disabilities
- Other practical information
- Further information
- Tourist information
- Admission charges: Expensive (over €6), Moderate (€3–€6) and Inexpensive (€3 or less)
- Major Sight
- Minor Sight
- Walks
- Excursions
- Shops
- Entertainment and Nightlife
- Restaurants

This guide is divided into four sections

• Essential Lisbon: An introduction to the city and tips on making the most of your stay.

• Lisbon by Area: We've broken the city into six areas, and recommended the best sights, shops, entertainment venues, nightlife and restaurants in each one. Suggested walks help you to explore on foot.

• Where to Stay: The best hotels, whether you're looking for luxury, budget or something in between.

• Need to Know: The info you need to make your trip run smoothly, including getting about by public transport, weather tips, emergency phone numbers and useful websites.

Navigation In the Lisbon by Area chapter, we've given each area its own tint, which is also used on the locator maps throughout the book and the map on the inside front cover.

Maps The fold-out map accompanying this book is a comprehensive street plan of Lisbon. The grid on this fold-out map is the same as the grid on the locator maps within the book. We've given grid references within the book for each sight and listing.

Contents

ESSENTIAL LISBON 4–18

Introducing Lisbon 4–5
A Short Stay in Lisbon 6–7
Top 25 8–9
Shopping 10–11
Shopping by Theme 12
Lisbon by Night 13
Eating Out 14
Restaurants by Cuisine 15
If You Like... 16–18

LISBON BY AREA 19–106

BAIXA-CHIADO 20–38

Area Map 22–23
Sights 24–30
Walk 31
Shopping 32–35
Entertainment and Nightlife 36
Restaurants 36–38

MOURARIA-ALFAMA 39–54

Area Map 40–41
Sights 42–51
Walk 52
Shopping 53
Entertainment and Nightlife 53
Restaurants 54

BAIRRO ALTO/THE WEST 55–72

Area Map 56–57
Sights 58–64
Tour 65
Shopping 66
Entertainment and Nightlife 67–68
Restaurants 69–72

SÃO SEBASTIÃO 73–82

Area Map 74–75
Sights 76–82

BELÉM 83–96

Area Map 84–85
Sights 86–95
Restaurants 96

FARTHER AFIELD 97–106

Area Map 98–99
Sights 100–105
Excursions 106

WHERE TO STAY 107–112

Introduction 108
Budget Hotels 109
Mid-Range Hotels 110–111
Luxury Hotels 112

NEED TO KNOW 113–125

Planning Ahead 114–115
Getting There 116–117
Getting Around 118–119
Essential Facts 120–121
Language 122–123
Timeline 124–125

Introducing Lisbon

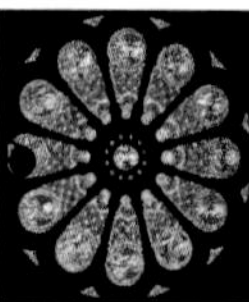

Lisbon is a perfect medley of old and new, a glorious remnant of a once-powerful maritime empire mixed with a dynamic, forward-looking city of considerable cultural and social élan. This previously moribund capital has evolved into a modern city.

You need not fear, for while shaking off the worst of the past, the city has retained much of the quirky and unpretentious charm that makes it such a pleasure to visit. Modern office buildings and shopping malls may sprout across the city, muscling in on an atmospheric medley of Moorish and medieval quarters, but in their shadow you will still find streets full of rattling old trams, crumbling mansions, walls of beautiful tiles, mosaic pavements, lovely churches, festive markets and any number of glorious old bars and cafés, where the traditional conversational certainties of football, family and religion still hold sway.

The social and cultural changes wrought by greater prosperity have made their mark in Lisbon. The city's new cultural swagger was first made manifest on a grand scale in 1994, when Lisbon was named a European City of Culture, and continues today in dazzling cultural complexes such as the Centro Cultural de Belém (▷ 94). It's also apparent in the new funky shops and smart galleries of contemporary art in the Bairro Alto and elsewhere, and in the city's artists and brash young fashion designers, who confidently show their work in London, Paris and New York.

Lisbon's transformation has been dramatic and quick, and in the wrench that has pulled it virtually from the 19th to the 21st century in less than a generation, some people—and places—have inevitably been left behind. At the same time, it is clearly a city on the move, and one where you sense that things can only get better—but also one where you can rest assured that the old charm will never entirely disappear.

Facts + Figures

- **Lisbon is Europe's most westerly city.**
- **The population of Lisbon is about 536,000. The population of Greater Lisbon and the Tagus valley is around 3,327,000—about a third of Portugal's total population.**

TRAMS

A great way to see contemporary Lisbon is on one of the city's oldest means of public transport. Trams have been rattling around Lisbon's streets since 1901. Today they run on 72km (45 miles) of track. Take the 28 tram for a memorable sightseeing tour, or the 15 from Praça da Figueira to Belém for a look at one of the city's modern super-trams.

TILES

Tiles, or *azulejos*, are found almost everywhere in Lisbon. '*Azulejos*' comes from the Arab word *al azulaycha*, meaning 'polished little stone'. The Moors introduced the tile-making art to the Iberian peninsula in the eighth century. Tiles are still used in many contemporary buildings, notably the Cais do Sodré and other metro stations.

MODERN CITY

Lisbon's stunning contemporary architecture includes the Armazéns do Chiado (▷ 32)—the stylish focal point of the Chiado district—and Peter Chermayeff's wondrous Oceanário, the Ponte Vasco da Gama and Álvaro Siza Vieira's extraordinary curved concrete roof for the Pavilhão de Portugal. These architectural marvels can be located at the Parque das Nações (▷ 103), designed for the 1998 World Expo.

A Short Stay in Lisbon

DAY 1

Morning Start your day in the medieval district of Lisbon, the **Alfama** (▷ 42–43). Walk or take tram 12 or 28 up to the **Sé** (▷ 48–49), Lisbon's imposing cathedral. Go up to the **Miradoura de Santa Luzia**—you can take a tram—for splendid views over the harbour.

Mid-morning Stop for a coffee at the **Café Cerca Moura** (▷ 54), close by the mirador. Continue up to visit the **Museu das Artes Decorativas** (▷ 45), housed in a beautiful 17th-century palace. Cut up the steep streets behind the museum to reach the **Castelo de São Jorge** (▷ 46).

Lunch You can take lunch in the castle grounds or alternatively wander down the narrow streets of the Alfama to eat later. Walk or take a tram down to **Praça do Comércio** (▷ 26), where you can have a snack in the popular **Café Martinho da Arcada** (▷ 36) or an expensive seafood lunch at **Terreiro do Paço** (▷ 38).

Afternoon From the square take the fast tram 15 to visit the Belém district. Get off at the stop after the monastery, so you can start your visit at the gem of a building, the **Torre de Belém** (▷ 92–93). You can then board the open-air mini-train, which takes you to all the scattered sights of Belém, or go on by foot. Highlights include the monument **Padrão dos Descobrimentos** (▷ 91), the **Museu de Marinha** (▷ 88–89), where you can stop for a coffee, the **Mosteiro dos Jerónimos** (▷ 86–87) and the **Museu Nacional dos Coches** (▷ 90).

Dinner Try the restaurant **Cais de Belém** (▷ 96), overlooking the park.

Evening Head back to town or take tram 15 or the train to the waterfront hot spot Alcântara, with its restaurants, bars and clubs.

DAY 2

Morning Start in **Praça do Comércio** (▷ 26) and walk through the arch to Rua Augusta to wander the grid of streets and check out the shopping. Head for Rua Áurea and let the **Elevador de Santa Justa** (▷ 30) whisk you up into Chiado, giving you great views. Walk up Rua do Carmo, with lots more shopping opportunities.

Mid-morning Continue on to Rua Garrett, pausing at Lisbon's most famous coffeehouse, **Café a Brasileira** (▷ 36). The streets to the north have some of the best shops in the city or you could visit the **Museu Arqueológico** (▷ 25) back in Largo do Carmo. Walk downhill, or take the elevator, and make your way to **Rossio** (▷ 27), Lisbon's central square.

Lunch Head to Rua das Portas de Santo Antão, just north of the square, for a choice of restaurants. Try **Casa do Alentejo** (▷ 37) for traditional fare or, for fish, the more expensive **Gambrinus** (▷ 38).

Afternoon Take the green line metro from Rossio and change at Alameda for the red line to Oriente. This brings you to the **Parque das Nações** (▷ 103), the site of Expo 98, with its excellent science museum and aquarium—great for kids. There is a lot to do and see here and you might want to stay on into the evening.

Dinner Have a meal at the Parque or head back to the **Bairro Alto** (▷ 58) to Rua do Diario de Noticias/Rua Atalaia area (Baixa-Chiado metro), with international restaurants such as the Argentinian **Último Tango** (▷ 72).

Evening This district is famous for its traditional *fado* music—try **Adega do Ribatejo** or **Adega do Machado** (▷ 67). This is also the place to go for bars, many of which feature live music and stay open very late.

Top 25

TOP 25

➤➤➤

Alfama ▷ 42–43 The old part of the city, with narrow streets and evocative cafés, set beneath the castle.

Bairro Alto ▷ 58 Once the haunt of artists, this district is a popular nightspot with its bars and restaurants.

Baixa ▷ 24 A grid of 18th-century streets running down from Rossio to the Praça do Comércio.

Torre de Belém ▷ 92–93 The attractive UNESCO Heritage site was built to protect Lisbon's harbour.

Shopping in Chiado ▷ 28–29 A lovely area with some of the most elegant shops and boutiques in Lisbon.

Sé ▷ 48–49 Imposing cathedral, rebuilt after the 1755 earthquake, but retaining some original features.

Rossio ▷ 27 Bustling central meeting place, perfect for people-watching, that has witnessed some turbulent times in the past.

Praça do Comércio ▷ 26 Majestic square by the waterfront, with a triumphal arch leading from the sea into the city.

Parque das Nações ▷ 103 Impressive and thriving cultural waterside development originally built for Expo 98.

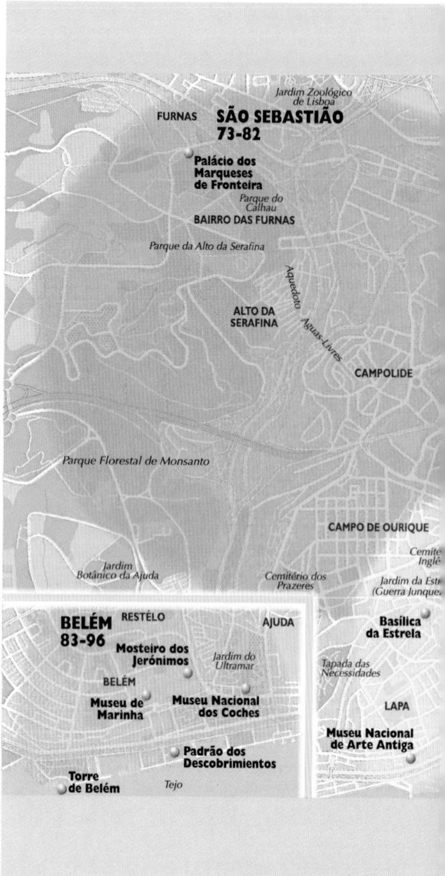

Palácio dos Marqueses de Fronteira ▷ 78–79 Lovely palace, just a metro ride away in the suburbs.

Padrão dos Descobrimentos ▷ 91 The monument reaches out towards the sea.

Museu Nacional dos Coches ▷ 90 Splendid coaches and carriages built for royalty and nobility.

These pages are a quick guide to the Top 25, which are described in more detail later. Here they are listed alphabetically, and the tinted background shows which area they are in.

Basílica da Estrela ▷ 59 Dominating the surrounding area, this impressive church affords great views.

Campo de Santa Clara ▷ 44 The striking church offers a fine backdrop for the weekly markets.

Castelo de São Jorge ▷ 46 You can't avoid seeing this fine castle from all over the city.

Centro de Arte Moderna ▷ 80 Get acquainted with Portuguese artists at this stylish gallery.

Igreja da Madre de Deus ▷ 100–101 A glittering golden extravaganza to the north of the Alfama district.

Igreja de São Roque ▷ 60–61 Wonderful collections of tiles and elaborate decoration in this church.

Mosteiro dos Jerónimos ▷ 86–87 Superb 16th-century monastery in Belém.

Museu Arqueológico do Carmo ▷ 25 Eccentric, but interesting collection.

Museu das Artes Decorativas ▷ 45 Beautiful 17th-century palace displaying a wonderful collection of objects.

Museu Calouste Gulbenkian ▷ 76–77 Portugal's single greatest museum.

Museu Nacional do Azulejo ▷ 102 Unique museum dedicated to the celebrated *azulejo,* or tile.

Museu Nacional de Arte Antiga ▷ 62–63 Fine collection of ancient art and decorative objects.

Museu de Marinha ▷ 88–89 The museum brings to life Portugal's naval history and love of the sea.

Shopping

Lisbon is not a shopper's haven compared with London, Paris or New York, but the city does score high for its range of traditional and specialist shops, and in its prices, which, for certain goods, notably shoes and leatherware, are some of the lowest in Western Europe. The city's gentle pace makes it an ideal place for relaxed browsing, but for a more dynamic experience visit one of the city's popular shopping malls.

Traditional Roots

The main shopping areas are easily defined. The key area has always been the Baixa, whose central grid of streets—unlike those of many modern cities—still retains a wonderful array of traditional and designer stores. Behind the tiny shopfronts, many with lovely art nouveau façades, you'll find everything from Louis Vuitton and La Perla to dusty cobblers and pungent old grocers' stores piled with cheeses, vintage port and other Portuguese staples. Many of the specialist shops here have been run by the same family of craftspeople for centuries.

Cutting-Edge Style

The steep narrow streets of the Bairro Alto district have an altogether more cutting-edge collection of shops, including many small designer fashion outlets, modern furniture showrooms and eccentric stores that reflect the area's chic, bohemian feel. Much the same can

SHOPPING CARD

Lisbon's Turismo de Lisboa offers various discount cards and other passes (▷ 118), including the Lisboa Shopping Card, offering between 5 and 15 per cent off in around 200 stores in the Baixa, Chiado, Avenida da Liberdade and other main shopping districts. Two versions, valid for 24 and 72 hours, cost €3.70 and €5.80 respectively (check latest price on website). They are available at all Turismo de Lisboa outlets (▷ 116). For information www.atl.turismolisboa.pt or www.askmelisboa.com.

You can pick up a souvenir of Lisbon at the excellent range of individual shops

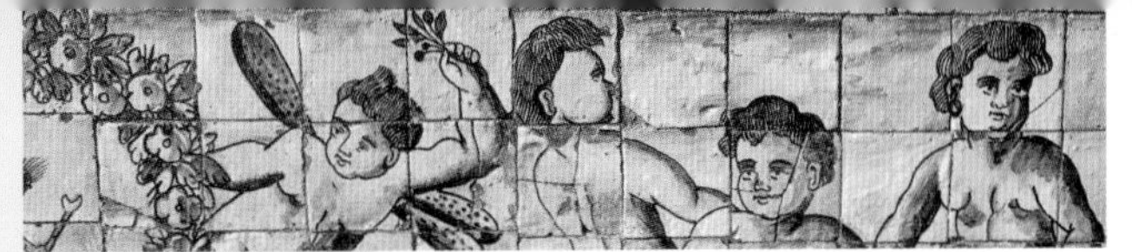

be said of the adjacent Chiado, though here the prices are higher and the stores more exclusive. Most big names appear on Avenida da Liberdade, with price tags rising the farther north you go.

Shopping Malls

Most of the shopping malls are more outlying, though this does nothing to deter *Lisboetas*, who seem to have taken modern malls to their hearts—the biggest and best are Amoreiras, Colombo and Centro Comercial Vasco da Gama (▷ 103). At the other extreme, Lisbon has plenty of down-to-earth street markets, many worth visiting as much for their local atmosphere as their bargains (▷ below).

Value for Money

As for Lisbon's best buys, shoes and leatherware are often inexpensive—though styles and sizes may be limited—as are some of the country's traditional foods and wines, not least the vintage port, which you'll often find, along with other foodstuffs, at good prices in the supermarkets. Tiles (*azulejos*) and ceramics are also good buys, and make excellent souvenirs to take home, as do wooden craft goods, linens and other textiles. Antiques are never inexpensive, but you'll find a good selection in and around the Bairro Alto, especially in the shops on Rua de São Bento and Rua Dom Pedro V.

MARKETS

One of Lisbon's most lively shopping experiences is the Feira da Ladra (🕑 Tue and Sat 7am–6.30pm), a flea market at Campo de Santa Clara in the Alfama district (▷ 44). Many stalls sell little more than junk, but there are also stalls with decent antiques, clothes, CDs, handicrafts and more. The best of the food and general markets is the Mercado Ribeira on Avenida 24 de Julho (▷ 66), a short walk from Cais do Sodré. Various theme markets take place each Sunday at the Parque das Nações (▷ 103), above the metro station, ranging from stamps and coins to handicrafts, antiques and decorative arts.

Shopping by Theme

Whether you're looking for a department store, a quirky boutique, or something in between, you'll find it all in Lisbon. On this page shops are listed by theme. For a more detailed write-up, see the individual listings in Lisbon by Area.

ACCESSORIES

Azevedo Rua (▷ 32)
Lord (▷ 34)
Luvaria Ulisses (▷ 34)

ANTIQUES

A Trindade (▷ 32)
M. Murteira (▷ 53)

BOOKS/MAPS

FNAC (▷ 33)
Livraria Bertrand (▷ 34)
Livraria Buchholz (▷ 66)
Tabacaria Mónaco (▷ 35)

CRAFTS/SOUVENIRS

Alberto Santos (▷ 32)
Artesanato do Tejo (▷ 32)
Casa de Bordados de Madeira (▷ 32)
Casa Havaneza (▷ 32)
Casa Maciel (▷ 33)
Casa Portuguesa (▷ 33)
Casa do Turista (▷ 33)
Casa das Velas do Loreto (▷ 66)
Santos Oficios (▷ 35)

FASHION

Alfaiataria Nunes Corrêa (▷ 32)
Ana Salazar (▷ 32)
El Dorado (▷ 66)
Fátima Lopes (▷ 66)
José António Tenente (▷ 34)
Storytailors (▷ 35)

FOOD/DRINK

A Carioca (▷ 32)
Adivinho (▷ 53)
Chá Casa Pereira (▷ 33)
Confeitaria Nacional (▷ 33)
Garrafeira Nacional (▷ 33)
Manuel Tavares (▷ 34)
Mercado Municipal de Santa Clara (▷ 53)
Mercado Ribeira (▷ 66)
Mercearia Liberdade (▷ 34)
Napoleão (▷ 34)
O Celeiro (▷ 35)

HOMEWARE

Arquitectónica (▷ 66)
Deposito da Marinha Grande (▷ 66)
Retrosaria Nardo (▷ 35)
Vista Alegre (▷ 35)

JEWELLERY

Joalharia do Carmo (▷ 34)
Sarmento (▷ 35)

LINENS

Madeira House (▷ 34)
Paris em Lisboa (▷ 35)
Príncipe Real (▷ 66)
Teresa Alecrim (▷ 35)

MALLS

Amoreiras (▷ 66)
Armazéns do Chiado (▷ 32)

TILES

Fábrica de Céramica Viúva Lamego (▷ 53)
Fábrica Sant'Anna (▷ 33)

Lisbon by Night

Atmospheric Lisbon by night—from traditional fado *haunts to the most modern of venues*

Not so long ago, nightlife in Lisbon consisted of little more than a handful of old bars, restaurants and the occasional live entertainment in the shape of *fado* (▷ 53). But as the rest of the city has changed, so has its nightlife, and today Lisbon has a huge selection of cutting-edge bars and state-of-the-art discos, as well as one of Europe's most dynamic clubbing scenes.

Where to Party

Much of the action takes place on the Bairro Alto, whose many sleek bars, clubs and lounges heave with up to 50,000 people on the busiest evenings of the week. As the night wears on, many of these revellers drift west to the clubs on Avenida 24 de Julho, or to the Alcântara, a rejuvenated dock area whose waterfront—especially the Doca de Santo Amaro—has been almost entirely given over to late-opening, warehouse-style bars and clubs. Clubbers have also moved east, to the even newer nightlife districts of the Parque das Nações (▷ 103) and Santa Apolónia waterfront.

A Little More Sedate

City nightlife need not be a frantic round of clubs. There are occasional opera and other classical music concerts, many staged outdoors when the weather allows. And on a summer evening, of course, nightlife need consist of no more than a relaxing meal under the stars, a quiet drink in an atmospheric bar or a balmy evening stroll through some of the old city's more sedate streets.

NIGHTLIFE ETIQUETTE

Lisbon's bar and club scene does not really get going until midnight. Many clubs have an admission charge—anything up to €30—which might include one or two drinks (admission may be free on quieter weekdays). On entry, there may also be a *consumo mínimo*, or minimum consumption charge. Bouncers can refuse admission if the club is full, or if you are underdressed.

Eating Out

Portugal has suffered a bad press where cuisine is concerned, with many a menu unchanged for more than 30 years. However, with a more cosmopolitan approach to life, Lisbon is seeing a change in cooking, albeit with the traditional components remaining intact.

Eat out under the blue sky, on a shaded terrace or in a garden, or indoors in traditional surroundings

Portuguese Roots

There is a tradition of simple, wholesome food in the country and this is retained in many recipes today. Fish lies at the heart, with seafood and fresh fish as popular as ever. With all that fresh fish available, it is perhaps difficult to understand the Portuguese love of the ubiquitous *bacalhau* (dried salt cod). It was first introduced way back when the Portuguese caught the cod off the shores of Newfoundland, bringing it home to be salted, dried and preserved. There is said to be a recipe for *bacalhau* for each day of the year. You will come across many traditional dishes in Lisbon, but they are increasingly produced in a more innovative way.

Eating Times

Start the day as the *Lisboetas* do, with a pastry and strong coffee, standing up at the bar in true European style. Lunch is a robust affair, usually taken between 12.30 and 2pm. This should keep you going until dinner, which is often not taken until 8pm (or later at the weekend), but you will find tourists packing the restaurants as early as 7pm.

SARDINES

This humble fish is close to the hearts of the people of Portugal and in Lisbon the beginning of summer is heralded by the opening of the sardine season. With the onset of the warmer nights and the celebration of the patron saint of Lisbon, St. Anthony, on 13 June, grilled sardines become a focal point. Eaten with boiled potatoes and salad, and often served on a piece of bread, they are washed down with white *vinho verde*, red wine or beer.

Restaurants by Cuisine

There are restaurants to suit all tastes and budgets in Lisbon. On this page they are listed by cuisine. For a more detailed description of each restaurant, see Lisbon by Area.

CAFÉS/*PASTELARIAS*

Antiga Casa dos Pastéis de Belém (▷ 96)
Café a Brasileira (▷ 36)
Café Cerca Moura (▷ 54)
Café Martinho da Arcada (▷ 36)
Café Nicola (▷ 37)
Casa Chineza (▷ 37)
Confeitaria Nacional (▷ 37)
Cultura do Chá (▷ 71)
O Chá da Lapa (▷ 71)
Pastelaria Bénard (▷ 38)
Pastelaria Suiça (▷ 38)

FINE DINING

Casa da Comida (▷ 69)
Confraria at York House (▷ 71)
Conventual (▷ 71)
Restaurante 33 (▷ 72)
Tágide (▷ 38)
Tavares (▷ 38)
Terreiro do Paço (▷ 38)
Vela Latina (▷ 96)

INTERNATIONAL

Ali-à-Papa (▷ 69)
Casanova (▷ 54)
Clube dos Jornalistas (▷ 69)
Comida de Santo (▷ 69)
Delhi Palace (▷ 54)
Picanha (▷ 72)
Último Tango (▷ 72)

LIGHT MEALS/SNACKS

Alfaia (▷ 69)
Bonjardim (▷ 36)
Café no Chiado (▷ 37)
Casa Faz Frio (▷ 69)
Enoteca Chafariz do Vinho (▷ 71)
Portugália (▷ 72)

MOST FASHIONABLE

Bica do Sapato (▷ 54)
Espaço Lisboa (▷ 71)
L'Entrecote (▷ 37)
Solar dos Nunes (▷ 72)
XL (▷ 72)

SEAFOOD

Cais da Ribeira (▷ 38)
Cervejaria Pinóquio (▷ 37)
Faz Figura (▷ 54)
Fidalgo (▷ 71)
Gambrinus (▷ 38)
Mercado do Peixe (▷ 96)
Ribadouro (▷ 72)
Solmar (▷ 38)

TRADITIONAL

BBC (▷ 96)
Bota Alta (▷ 69)
Cais de Belém (▷ 96)
Casa do Alentejo (▷ 37)
Cervejaria Trindade (▷ 37)
Lautasco (▷ 54)
Malmequer Bemmequer (▷ 54)
O Carvoeiro (▷ 96)
O Caseiro (▷ 96)
Olivier (▷ 71)
Pap'açorda (▷ 72)
Primavera (▷ 72)
Via Graça (▷ 54)

If You Like...

However you'd like to spend your time in Lisbon, these top suggestions should help you tailor your ideal visit. Each sight or listing has a fuller write-up elsewhere in the book.

PORTUGUESE CUISINE

For food from the Alentejo region try Casa do Alentejo (▷ 37).
Sample *bacalhau* (salt cod) at authentic Olivier (▷ 71), renowned for this traditional dish.
Inexpensive but tasty traditional fare can be found at Malmequer Bemmequer (▷ 54).

HISTORIC CAFÉS

The most famous of all is the Café a Brasileira (▷ 36) in the Bairro Alto.
Café Nicola (▷ 37) has been serving customers since 1777.
One of Lisbon's finest cafés is Pastelaria Bénard (▷ 38)—try the desserts.

Lisbon is a great place to eat fish (top); Café Nicola, a popular haunt (above)

A PALATIAL STAY

Palácio de Belmonte (▷ 112) is one of the world's finest small hotels.
Stay at a historic hotel like Pestana Palace (▷ 112), set in fabulous grounds.
Stay in Sintra among the luxury of the Palácio de Seteais (▷ 112).

LISBON ON A BUDGET

Stay in a pension such as Pensão São João de Praça (▷ 109).
Big portions are the order of the day at low-price Bota Alta restaurant (▷ 69).
Visit the Museu Calouste Gulbenkian, Lisbon's greatest museum, on a Sunday—it's free (▷ 76–77).

Palácio de Belmonte (above right); a piece of Chinese porcelain from the dynasty of Ts'ing in the Gulbenkian Museum (right)

he Jardim Guerra unqueiro for erfect eace

A RELAXING BREAK

Enjoy the views and the exotic birds in the gardens of the Castelo de São Jorge (▷ 46–47).

An oasis of calm can be found in the Jardim Botãnico (▷ 64).

Take a rest while the kids play in the spacious grounds of the Jardim Guerra Junqueiro (▷ 64).

BUYING SOUVENIRS

A tipple of port from its natural home can be bought from Napoleão in the Baixa (▷ 34).

Portuguese handicrafts of all kinds are for sale at Alberto Santos (▷ 32).

For all things nostalgic go to Casa Portuguesa (▷ 33).

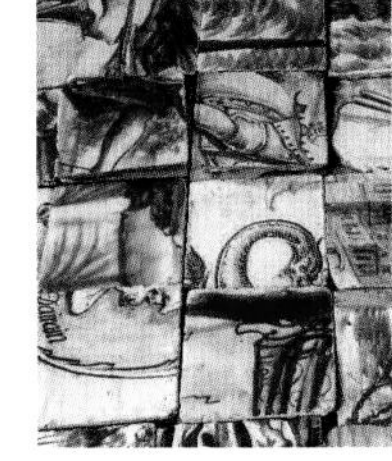

Port and tiles make ideal gifts (above)

TRADITIONAL TILES

The best choice of *azulejos* (tiles) to buy is at Viúva Lamego (▷ 53).

The leading producer of tiles since 1741 has been Fábrica Sant'Anna (▷ 33), located in the Alfama district.

RIDING HIGH

The Elevador de Santa Justa (▷ 30) will whisk you up to the Bairro Alto.

For another route up to Bairro Alto take the Elevador da Glória (▷ 58).

Take the cable car and ride high over the Parque das Nações (▷ 103) for a view of the whole park.

Get a bird's-eye view from the cable car at Parque das Nações (left)

GOOD PLACES TO AMUSE THE CHILDREN

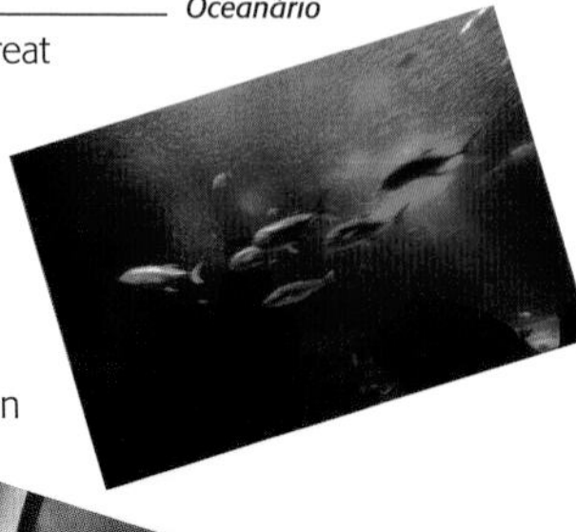

See what lurks in the deep blue sea at Oceanário

Oceanário (▷ 105) is just one of the great attractions for kids in the Parque das Nações (▷ 103).

Budding sailors will enjoy the Museu de Marinha maritime museum at Belém (▷ 88–89).

Special sky shows for children take place at the Planetário Calouste Gulbenkian (▷ 94).

TRADITIONAL MUSIC

Get to know *fado* music at the popular tourist spot Clube de Fado (▷ 53) or O Sr Vinho (▷ 68).

For *fado* and a meal try the reasonably priced Parreirinha de Alfama (▷ 53).

Music and traditional folklore can be found at the historic Café Luso (▷ 67).

A TRENDY NIGHT-TIME SCENE

Ultratrendy Lux (▷ 53) is the place to be seen, with great views over the river from the terrace.

For the most eccentric bar in town try the Pavilhão Chinês (▷ 68) with its walls crammed with wierd and wonderful objects.

Hot Clube Jazz (▷ 67) is the best-known and revered jazz venue in the city.

Fado *and jazz houses are plentiful in Lisbon*

TRIPS FARTHER OUT

Parque das Nações (▷ 103) will keep you entertained for a full day.

If you want beautiful scenery and fabulous palaces go to Sintra (▷ 106).

Climb to the top of the Cristo Rei (▷ 65), on the other side of the Tejo River.

Castelo dos Mouros, looking down to the town of Sintra

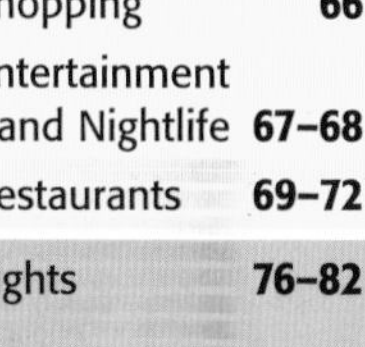

BAIXA-CHIADO

Sights 24–30
Walk 31
Shopping 32–35
Entertainment and Nightlife 36
Restaurants 36–38

MOURARIA/ALFAMA

Sights 42–51
Walk 52
Shopping 53
Entertainment and Nightlife 53
Restaurants 54

BAIRRO ALTO/THE WEST

Sights 58–64
Tour 65
Shopping 66
Entertainment and Nightlife 67–68
Restaurants 69–72

SÃO SEBASTIÃO

Sights 76–82

BELÉM

Sights 86–95
Restaurants 96

FARTHER AFIELD

Sights 100–105
Excursions 106

An inspired example of 18th-century town-grid planning, Baixa changed the face of the city. Spreading up the hill to the west, Chiado is home to museums, theatres, historic buildings, cafés and elegant shops.

Sights	24–30
Walk	31
Shopping	32–35
Entertainment and Nightlife	36
Restaurants	36–38

Top 25 TOP 25

Baixa ▷ **24**
Museu Arqueológico do Carmo ▷ **25**
Praça do Comércio ▷ **26**
Rossio ▷ **27**
Shopping in Chiado ▷ **28**

5
6
7
8
9
G
H
J
Hospital de Santo António dos Capuchos
AVENIDA DA LIBERDADE
Rua J Cesar Machado
Rua de São José
Rua do Passadiço
Rua St A d Capuchos
Rua da Fe
Rua do Telhal
Rua J Andrade
Avenida
Avenida da Liberdade
Largo d Anunciada
C do Lavra
Rua d Portas d S A
Museu Etnológico da Sociedade de Geografia
Colis
Praça dos Restauradores
Palácio Foz
Restauradores
Largo Domir
Largo D Cadaval
ESTAÇÃO CENTRAL DO ROSSIO
RUA D MISERICÓRDIA
Rua Nova d Trindade
Rua d Condessa
Rua da Oliveira
Museu Arqueológio do Carmo
CHIADO
Rua Garrett
Rua Cardoso
Rua Capelo
Rua A Maria
Rua D de Bragança
Serpa Pinto
Largo Bibliot Púb
Museu do Chiado
Rua Victor Córdon
RUA DO ALECRIM
Rua Nova do Carvalho
Rua do Arsen
Ministé
Praça D da Terceira
AVENIDA DA RIBEIR
Cais do Sodré
Gare Fluvial
0
250 m
0
250 yds

Rua C A Pedroso
ANJOS
Rua de São Lázaro
Pátria
Hospital de São José
Rua M Vaz
RUA DA PALMA
Rua da Mourania
Teatro Dona Maria II
R D DUARTE
Rossio
Rossio
Praça da Figueira
Praça Dom Pedro IV
RUA DA BETESGA
Elevador de Santa Justa
RUA DOS
RUA DA PRATA
Rua dos Correeiros
Rua Augusta
Rua dos Douradores
Rua dos Fanqueiros
Rua de São Mamede
Rua da Madalena
Baixa-Chiado
RUA AUREA
Rua N do Almada
Rua do Crucifixo
Rua Sapateiros
Rua d Vitória
BAIXA
Rua de Conceição
São Julião
Rua do Comércio
Ministérios
Praça do Município
Praça do Comércio
Ministérios
AVENIDA INFANTE DOM HENRIQUE
Welcome Center
Cais das Colunas
DAS NAUS
Estação Fluvial Terreiro do Paço
Tejo
K
L

Baixa

Art deco shopfronts in the Baixa (left); an aerial view of the district at night (right)

THE BASICS

K7–K8
Streets between the Rossio and Praça do Comércio
Cafés, bars and restaurants
Rossio/Baixa-Chiado
All services to Rossio and Praça do Comércio
Poor

HIGHLIGHTS

- Art deco shopfronts
- Mosaic pavements
- Cobbled streets

The tiny Baixa district, with its network of 18th-century cobbled streets, its many elaborate shopfronts and lively commercial bustle, forms the heart of old Lisbon. It is lodged between the hills of the Chiado and Alfama.

Pombal's vision A grid of ordered streets, the Baixa district stretches from the Rossio in the north to the Praça do Comércio in the south, with the Chiado rising to the west and the Alfama to the east. It is thought this low-lying area was once on a stream, with houses built on stilts to escape flooding. Its appearance was changed beyond all recognition following the 1755 earthquake, when the Marquês de Pombal decided to rebuild the area along strictly rational lines. He decreed that all new streets should be '40 feet in width, with pavements on either side protected from wheeled traffic by stone pillars, as in London'.

Tradition Pombal's dream was realized with the help of a military engineer, Eugénio dos Santos, and the result has been described by some as one of the finest European architectural achievements of the age. To others, the district's relentless simplicity and symmetry made it appear bland and soulless. Today there is no denying the streets' lively old-fashioned charm, nor the appeal of the mosaic-patterned pavements, tiled façades and lovely old shopfronts. The pedestrianized Rua Augusta is the area's main axis. Many minor streets bear names relating to the trades once conducted there.

Housed in the ruins of a convent (left), the museum is just off Rossio square (right)

Museu Arqueológico do Carmo

Modern, well-organized museums such as the Gulbenkian are a joy, but there is something appealing about the wonderfully jumbled and eccentric collection of exhibits in the Museu Arqueológico do Carmo.

Location The archaeological museum is within the ruins of the Convento do Carmo, a Carmelite convent built by Nuno Álvares Pereira. He was a general and companion-in-arms to João I at the Battle of Aljubarrota in 1385, which secured Portuguese independence from Castile for 200 years. Until 1755, when the convent church was toppled by the Great Earthquake, it was the largest church in the city. Over the years its ruins were used as a graveyard and military stable. Today its soaring Gothic interior is largely open to the Lisbon sky, the nave and chancel now a threadbare garden full of cats, flowers and shattered statuary.

Eccentric The museum's exhibits are a slightly disorganized and eccentric mixture, though none the worse for that, their eclectic jumble constituting part of their appeal. They include two tombs, one belonging to Ferdinand I, King of Portugal from 1367 to 1382, the other to Gonçalo de Souza, chancellor to Henry the Navigator. The stone bust in the chancel is said to be the oldest known image of Afonso Henriques, Portugal's first king. Older exhibits include prehistoric and Visigothic objects, and more eccentric displays include shrunken heads, two South American mummies and many florid pieces of sculpture.

THE BASICS

www.museusportugal.org/aap

J7

Convento do Carmo, Largo do Carmo

213 478 629

May–end Sep Mon–Sat 10–6; Oct–end Apr Mon–Sat 10–5. Closed public hols

Baixa-Chiado

758; tram 28; Elevador de Santa Justa

Poor

Inexpensive

HIGHLIGHTS

- **Church ruins**
- **Shrunken heads**
- **Mummies**
- **Gothic tombs**
- **Bronze Age pottery**
- **Tiles**
- **Prehistoric objects**

Praça do Comércio

The Arco da Rua Augusta (left) dominates the arcaded Praça do Comércio

THE BASICS

- K8
- Praça do Comércio
- Terreiro do Paço/Baixa-Chiado
- All services to Praça do Comércio
- Good
- Free

HIGHLIGHTS

- View from the waterfront
- Triumphal arch
- Arcades
- Statue of Dom José I

The Praça do Comércio, the focus of the Marquês de Pombal's reconstruction of 1758, is dominated by the statue of José I. It provides a triumphal entrance to the city from the airy open spaces of the waterfront.

Gateway Locally, the square is known as the Terreiro do Paço, or Terrace of the Palace, an allusion to the 16th-century Royal Palace that stood here until it was almost completely destroyed by the 1755 earthquake. At its heart stands an equestrian statue of José I, king at the time of the 1755 earthquake, the blackened tone of its bronze giving rise to the Praça's nickname 'Black Horse Square'. It took some 1,000 people almost four days to move the statue into position. The palace's old steps still climb up from the waterfront, but today the square is dominated by the vast, 19th-century triumphal arch on its northern flank, and by ranks of imposing arcades and neoclassical government offices. In 1908, King Carlos I was assassinated together with Luis Filipe, his son and heir, in the corner of the square near Rua do Arsenal.

Revival Now that the city authorities have banned its use as a parking lot, the Praça do Comércio is once again one of Lisbon's most majestic squares. Its grand spaces and imposing buildings, once compromised, have been released from the motorcar's tyranny and the square can again reveal its intended effect—to serve as a dramatic gateway from the sea, and as an antechamber to the well-ordered streets of the Baixa and the rest of the city.

Shopping, relaxing, people-watching—it's what Lisbon's busiest square is all about

Rossio

Every city has its main square, and Lisbon's is the Rossio. Though it is not the prettiest place to take a break—there is little greenery and a lot of traffic—it does appeal as a meeting place for visitors and locals alike.

Turbulent past The Rossio, also known as Praça Dom Pedro IV, is Lisbon's natural focus, a large and bustling square close to one of the city's main stations, the Chiado shopping district and the Baixa. It dates from around the 13th century, though its present appearance is due mostly to the Marquês de Pombal, and 19th-century rebuilding. Between 1534 and 1820 the Inquisitors' palace stood on the north side, and in the 16th century the Inquisitors' victims—convicted heretics—were burned in the square. The Inquisition's sentences were handed down from São Domingos, a church to the east, still closed after a fire in the 1950s.

Relaxing present Today the square is lined with cafés and shops, some of which have fine elegant façades. Many of the cafés have outside tables, the best vantage points from which to watch the world go by. The statue on the 23m (75.5ft) marble pillar (1870) at the heart of the square is a bronze statue of Dom Pedro IV; the four figures at the base represent Justice, Wisdom, Courage and Restraint—attributes ascribed to the king. The square's grandest building, the Teatro Nacional Dona Maria II (▷ 36), was built in the 1840s on the site of the former Inquisitors' palace.

THE BASICS

- K7
- Praça Dom Pedro IV
- Cafés, bars and restaurants
- Rossio
- All services to Rossio
- Poor

HIGHLIGHTS

- Cafés
- Shopfronts
- Statue of Dom Pedro IV
- Fountain
- Teatro Nacional
- Façade of Estação do Rossio (station)

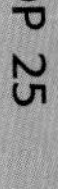

Shopping in Chiado

TOP 25

HIGHLIGHTS

- Rua Garrett
- Teatro de São Carlos
- Igreja dos Mártires
- Museu Arqueológico do Carmo (▷ 25)
- Café A Brasileira
- Museu do Chiado (▷ 30)

TIP

- Check out Armazéns do Chiado (▷ 32), where you can do all your shopping under one roof, then choose one of the eating options on the top floor for lunch.

Despite its damage by fire in 1988, today the Chiado thrives. Modern boutiques and department stores, hidden behind beautifully restored façades, sit harmoniously beside Lisbon's oldest shops.

District The Chiado is one of the five loosely defined districts that make up the heart of old Lisbon. Named after the poet António Ribeiro, who was nicknamed O Chiado, meaning 'Squeaky', it lies just alongside the Baixa, spreading across the first of the slopes that rise westward to the Bairro Alto. Known primarily as a shopping district, it embraces not only the main Largo do Chiado, but also a range of streets around the Rua Garrett and Rua do Carmo. Affluent and fashionable, its streets contain many luxury shops and fine old cafés, notably A Brasileira (▷ 36) in Rua Garrett. Also here are the

Step inside the gorgeous Café a Brasileira in the heart of Chiado to see its gilded mirrors and dark-wood panels (left); you can join poet Fernando Pessoa on a seat outside the café—perfect on a warm summer's day (middle); elaborate decoration on a façade in the Chiado district (right)

Teatro Nacional de São Carlos (▷ 36) opera house and the Igreja dos Mártires, the latter built over the site of a Crusader burial ground and encampment.

Destruction On 25 August 1988 the Chiado achieved unwanted fame when it was ravaged by fire. The conflagration is thought to have started in a store on Rua do Carmo, and devastated four blocks of the district before being brought under control. Some 2,000 people lost their jobs, and many old buildings were gutted, including the famous Ferrari coffeehouse and Grandella department store. In the disaster's aftermath the Mayor of Lisbon entrusted the reconstruction of the area to Alvaro Siza Vieira, a celebrated Portuguese architect, who resolved to rebuild the district to a classical plan in keeping with the existing structures. This has now been successfully completed.

THE BASICS

- J8
- Streets between Rua do Carmo and Rua do Alecrim
- Cafés, bars and restaurants
- Baixa-Chiado
- 758, 790; tram 28
- Poor

More to See

AVENIDA DA LIBERDADE

Avenida da Liberdade cuts a 1,500m (1,650-yard), tree-lined swathe from the Rossio north to the Praça Marquês de Pombal junction, where Parque Eduardo VII begins. Lisbon's grandest road inevitably invites comparison with the Champs-Élysées in Paris. Though no peaceful green oasis, it is worth a stroll for its trees, water features, pavement mosaics, 19th-century buildings and outdoor cafés.

H5–J6 Avenida da Liberdade Restauradores, Avenida, Marquês de Pombal 36, 44, 91, 711, 732, 745

ELEVADOR DE SANTA JUSTA

Designed by Raul Mésnier du Ponsard, apprentice to Gustave Eiffel, this wonderfully eccentric iron structure whisks you 45m (148ft) up to Rua do Carmo, giving great views across the Baixa to Castelo de São Jorge, north to the central squares and south to the river.

K7 Rua Áurea to Rua do Carmo 213 613 000 7am–9pm Baixa–Chiado All services to Rossio; tram 28 Inexpensive

MUSEU DO CHIADO

www.museudochiado-ipmuseus.pt

In a 13th-century abbey, this museum is devoted to Portuguese painting and sculpture. It was refurbished in 1994 with dramatic high brick vaults and polished grey marble by the French architect Jean-Michel Wilmotte. Mostly focusing on the years 1850–1950, it delves into realism, romanticism, symbolism and modernism. Worth seeing are *A Sesta* by Almada Negreiros; *Lisboa e o Tejo* by Carlos Botelho; and Soares dos Reis's *O Desterrado.*

J8 Rua Serpa Pinto 4 213 432 148/9 Tue–Sun 10–6 Café Baixa–Chiado 758; tram 28 Moderate. Free Sun and public hols until 2

MUSEU ETNOLÓGICO DA SOCIEDADE DE GEOGRAFIA

This little gem in the middle of the city displays objects from Portugal's former colonies in Africa and Asia, in a remarkable late 19th-century room.

J6 Rua das Portas de Santo Antão 100 213 425 068 Call to book visit Restauradores 36, 44, 91, 711 Free

Tree-lined Avenida da Liberdade

A trip on the Elevador de Santa Justa offers great views

Chiado District

This is not a long walk, but it can be extended to take in the maze of streets of the Bairro Alto to the north and west.

DISTANCE: 2km (1.2 miles) **ALLOW:** 2 hours with visits

START

ROSSIO

K7 Rossio

❶ Begin in Rossio (▷ 27), also known as Praça Dom Pedro IV, and take the pedestrianized Rua do Carmo uphill. On your left you pass the Elevador de Santa Justa (▷ 30).

❷ Turn right into Rua Garrett, the Chiado's most prestigious street. Walk to the top and note the statue of poet Fernando Pessoa and the Café a Brasileira (▷ 36) on the right.

❸ Turn back down Rua Garrett a short way and a few doors to the left on the same side of the street is the equally revered Pastelaria Bénard (▷ 38).

❹ Here you will find the 12th-century church, Igreja dos Mártires. Take Rua Serpa Pinto to the right of the church and walk down past the Teatro Nacional de São Carlos (▷ 36).

❺ Continue past the hospital. You can visit the Museu do Chiado (▷ 30).

❻ Continue to the bottom of the street. Turn right and then right again to double-back up to Rua Garrett. Turn left into Largo do Chiado, right up Rua Misericórdia and take the first right at Largo da Trindade.

❼ Turn right and left to follow Rua da Trindade to the Largo do Carmo, with its ruined church and museum. Return to Rua da Oliveira in the northeast corner of the square, walk to the end and turn right down the steps, for views of the Baixa (▷ 24) and the *castelo* (▷ 46).

❽ Follow the steps down past the station and cross Rua 1 de Dezembro to return to Rossio and enjoy a well-deserved café break.

END

ROSSIO

K7 Rossio

Shopping

A CARIOCA

From behind a lovely art nouveau shopfront, A Carioca has been providing superb tea and coffee to Lisbon since 1937. The blends come from around the world.

J7 Rua da Misericórdia 9 213 420 377 Baixa-Chiado 758; tram 28

ALBERTO SANTOS

One of the oldest handicraft shops in Lisbon (opened in the 1960s), with an assortment of genuine handmade articles displayed in large showrooms a block down from the post office.

J7 Praça dos Restauradores 64 213 477 875 Restauradores

ALFAIATARIA NUNES CORRÊA

For top-quality tailoring drop by this reputable men's outfitter, whose claim to fame is that it once clothed the Portuguese royal family.

K8 Rua Augusta 250 213 240 930 Rossio/ Baixa-Chiado All services to Praça do Comércio or Rossio

ANA SALAZAR

www.anasalazar.pt

Ana Salazar is perhaps the best-known Portuguese fashion designer on the international stage. She is known primarily for her daring designs, and for special stretch fabrics. Currently she has two outlets in the city. The most central is the shop on Rua do Carmo, in the Chiado.

J7 Rua do Carmo 87 213 472 289 Rossio All services to Rossio

ANTÓNIO TRINDADE

As well as having a fine collection of antique porcelain and religious art, this antique shop on the Rua do Alecrim specializes in antique furniture.

J8 Rua do Alecrim 79–81 213 424 660 Baixa-Chiado

ARMAZÉNS DO CHIADO

www.armazensdochiado.com

A modern space over six floors, the Armazéns shopping area has high-street names and a large FNAC store, while the top floor is given over to eateries and a hotel.

J7 Rua do Carmo 2 213 210 600 Rossio All services to Rossio

SOAP BOX

Not many associate Portugal with the production of soap but the Portuguese have been hand-crafting fine soap since the 19th century. A range of exotically scented soaps packaged in exquisite art deco-style boxes (which make a great change from the usual ceramic gifts) are available—amongst others—at Napoleão, Rua da Conceição 16, in the Baixa and Mercearia da Atalaia, Rua da Atalaia 64, in the Bairro Alto.

ARTESANATO DO TEJO

Displayed inside the Lisboa Welcome Centre, Artesanato sells traditional and urban arts from the Lisbon region, ranging from kiln-baked ceramics and paintings to woven pieces and bobbin lace.

K8 Rua do Arsenal 25 210 312 820 Baxia-Chiado Tram 15, 18

AZEVEDO RUA

This splendid hat shop, founded in 1886, has every type of hat you can imagine. The large range is elegantly displayed in wooden cabinets beneath a stuccoed ceiling.

K7 Praça Dom Pedro IV 69–73 213 427 511 Rossio All services to Rossio

CASA DE BORDADOS DE MADEIRA

Inside the Avenida Palace hotel, this shop sells embroideries from Viana do Castelo and Madeira (expensive) and the famous fishermen's sweaters from Póvoa do Varzim.

J7 Rua 1 de Dezembro 137 213 421 447 Restauradores All services to Avenida da Liberdade

CASA HAVANEZA

Casa Havaneza, established in 1861, is devoted to the art of cigar making. If you insist on only the finest Havana cigars, this lovely little shop will

certainly fulfil your needs.
J8 Largo do Chiado 24 213 420 340 Baixa-Chiado 758; tram 28

CASA MACIEL

Lisbon is full of long-established shops: this one was founded in 1810, and has grown from a small metal-working factory into an award-winning outlet for all manner of beautifully crafted work in metal. Pieces can be made to individual designs if required.
J7 Rua da Misericórdia 63–65 213 422 451 Rossio 758; tram 28

CASA PORTUGUESA

You will find nostalgia in abundance at this treasure trove of all things traditional and Portuguese. From Couto toothpaste and Encerite wax to Viana de Castelo embroidery.
J8 Rua Anchieta 11 213 465 073 Baixa-Chiado 758; tram 28

CASA DO TURISTA

This shop does sell a selection of tacky souvenirs but it also has some tasteful regional clothing and accessories, including sweaters from Póvoa do Varzim near Oporto and scarves from the Minho.
J6 Avenida da Liberdade 159 213 151 558 Rossio/Avenida All services to Avenida da Liberdade

CHÁ CASA PEREIRA

This family-run shop, founded in 1930, sells teas and coffees blended and ground to your own taste. Other tempting items include vintage port and mouth-watering chocolates.
J8 Rua Garrett 38 213 426 694 Baixa-Chiado 758; tram 28

CONFEITARIA NACIONAL

www.confeitarianacional.com
In business since 1829, this bakery and confectioners are renowned for their excellent almond and egg-based sweets and traditional array of cookies. For fine views across the Praça da Figueira, head to the tea rooms on the first floor.
K7 Praça da Figueira 18B 213 424 470 Rossio

VINTAGE PORT

Vintage port—the best port—is made from the grapes of one year only, and then only if that year's harvest has been specially declared of vintage quality. It is bottled after two to four years in the cask and then ages for at least 10 years in the bottle. Since 1974, a port must have been bottled in Portugal to be called a vintage. Late-bottled port (LBV) is a port that is not quite up to vintage standard, but is still deemed good enough to mature in the bottle rather than the cask. Typically it is bottled after about four to six years. Crucially, port that ages in the bottle matures by reduction, turning a deep red. Port that ages in the cask matures through oxidation, and turns toward amber. The longer in the cask, the lighter the shade.

FÁBRICA SANT'ANNA

This historic company has been Portugal's leading producer of *azulejos*, or decorated tiles, since 1741. The Rua do Alecrim address is the shop for its beautifully decorated products, many of which are based on traditional designs. It is also possible to visit the main factory by prior arrangement.
J8 Rua do Alecrim 95–97 213 422 537 758; tram 28

FNAC

One of the many foreign retail chains to open in Lisbon over the past few years, FNAC has the most comprehensive selection of books (including a good range of foreign-language books), music and maps.
K8 Armazéns do Chiado, Loja 407; Rua do Carmo 2 707 313 435 Baixa-Chiado

GARRAFEIRA NACIONAL

www.garrafeiranacional.com
Founded in 1927, wine

enthusiasts will enjoy the museum atmosphere that enables you to sample some of the finest and rarest wines, such as a very rare port wine dating from 1795.
K7 Rua de Santa Justa 18 218 879 004 Rossio/Baixa-Chiado All services to Praça do Comércio or Rossio

HOSPITAL DAS BONECAS
Founded in 1830 as a dolls hospital, this small store specializes in repairing and selling dolls of all shapes and sizes. They also make dolls clothes so delightful that many are sold to dress premature babies.
K7 Praça da Figueira 7 213 428 574 Rossio

JOALHARIA DO CARMO
In business for almost a century, Joalharia do Carmo has few rivals when it comes to fine gold and silver filigree jewellery. It sells a wide variety of products, almost all of them handmade.
J7 Rua do Carmo 87b 213 424 200 Rossio All services to Rossio

JOSÉ ANTÓNIO TENENTE
José António Tenente opened his shop on Rua do Carmo in 1990. His exclusive lines are considered more conservative than other Bairro Alto boutiques.
J8 Travessa do Carmo 8 213 422 560 Baixa-Chiado

LIVRARIA BERTRAND
This charming old-fashioned shop, behind a blue-tiled façade, was founded in 1773 and is Lisbon's oldest bookshop. It carries a good selection of illustrated books on Lisbon and Portugal.
J8 Rua Garrett 17 213 476 122 Baixa-Chiado 758; tram 28

LORD
Behind an art deco-style façade is an atmosphere of yesteryear, where you will find a fine selection of hats and shoes for the well-dressed lady and gentleman.
K8 Rua Augusta 201 213 462 009 Rossio/Baixa-Chiado All services to Praça do Comércio or Rossio

LUVARIA ULISSES
This tiny shop is a treasure trove of gloves in every material imaginable, including silk, satin, lace, leather and cotton.
J7 Rua do Carmo 87/A 213 420 295 Rossio all services to Rossio

TILES GALORE

Azulejos have been decorating not only palaces, churches, chapels and public buildings for centuries but also the homes of Portugal, helping to waterproof against the winter rains. Very popular as souvenirs, you can find a vast array of fine hand-painted, antique and contemporary tiles to give to your friends or adorn your home.

MADEIRA HOUSE
www.madeira-house.com
This shop sells high-quality cottons, linens and gift items from the island of Madeira. It has two outlets, one in the Baixa and the other on the Avenida da Liberdade.
K8 Rua Augusta 131–135 213 426 813 Rossio/Baixa-Chiado All services to Praça do Comércio or Rossio

MANUEL TAVARES
www.manueltavares.com
For glorious food head to this shop in the Baixa, an institution for over 100 years.
K7 Rua da Betesga 1A/B 213 424 209 Rossio

MERCEARIA LIBERDADE
This shop is worth a visit for its centenary interior. It began business as a grocery store and retains all of its original fixtures now used to shelve ceramics, wines and other national crafts and produce.
J6 Avenida da Liberdade 207 213 547 046 Restauradores, Avenida

NAPOLEÃO
A must for port connoisseurs; you can have a taste before you buy. The

staff are knowledgeable and the vast selection is the best in Lisbon.
K8 Rua dos Fanqueiros 70 218 861 108 Baixa-Chiado, Rossio Tram 12, 28

O CELEIRO
www.celeiro-dieta.pt
O Celeiro sells natural foods, medicines, vitamins and cosmetics.
J7 Rua 1 de Dezembro 65 210 306 030 Rossio

PARIS EM LISBOA
At this Chiado landmark you can find all the quality Portuguese textile goods you need for the home, from bath robes through tea towels and bed linen.
J8 Rua Garrett 77 213 468 144 Baixa-Chiado

RETROSARIA NARDO
This haberdashers in the Baixa stocks a wide selection of buttons, ribbons, cords and threads.
K8 Rua da Conceição 62–64 213 421 350 Baixa-Chiado

SANTOS OFICIOS
This handicraft shop, founded in 1995, is inside a restored 18th-century stable. It sells handmade products from around the country, including ceramics, linens and sheepskin slippers.
K8 Rua da Madalena 87 218 872 031 Baixa-Chiado 37; tram 12, 28

SARMENTO
This family-run firm has been Lisbon's most prestigious jeweller for about a hundred years. The gold, silverware and filigree are some of the most exquisite in Portugal.
K8 Rua Áurea (Rua do Ouro) 251 213 426 774 Baixa-Chiado Tram 28

STORYTAILORS
www.storytailors.pt
Designers Luís Sanchez and João Branco have set up this charming studio, where they produce tailor-made and personalized women's clothing that shows great originality and detail, inspired by the haute-couture era.
J8 Calçada do Ferragial 8 213 432 306 Baixa-Chiado 758; tram 28

FASHION CAPITAL

Fashion designers are a relatively recent phenomenon in Lisbon (since the mid-1980s), but now with the help of such fashion events as the yearly *Moda Lisboa*, usually held in March or April, national designers are getting the publicity they deserve. From established names such as Fátima Lopes and Ana Salazar to the more recent talent of Maria Gambina and José António Tenente, Portuguese creations can now be found in shops and on the catwalks of Paris, London and Barcelona.

TABACARIA MÓNACO
This tiny newsagent and tobacconist is a Lisbon landmark. Founded in 1893, it preserves a wonderful art nouveau ambience, with a lovely tiled and painted interior. It is also a good place to come for maps, guides and foreign newspapers and magazines.
K7 Praça Dom Pedro IV 21 213 468 191 Rossio All services to Rossio No credit cards

TERESA ALECRIM
This shop is named after its owner, who produces fine high-quality embroideries created in either plain or patterned cotton in the Laura Ashley style. Pillowcases, sheets, towels and covers are but a few items she offers for sale.
K8 Rua Nova do Almada 76 213 421 831 Baixa-Chiado Tram 28

VISTA ALEGRE
www.vistaalegre.pt
In business since 1824, this prestigious firm is renowned in Portugal and beyond for its exquisite porcelain dinner sets and china. It supplied Portuguese royalty until 1910, and today still supplies china to many of the royal families of Europe. It also sells less expensive but still coveted tableware for everyday use.
J7 Largo do Chiado 20–23 213 461 401 Tram 28

Entertainment and Nightlife

COLISEU DOS RECREIOS

www.coliseulisboa.com
Everything from ballet and musicals to contemporary music.
J6 Rua Portas de Santo Antão 213 240 580 Restauradores

TEATRO MUNICIPAL DE SÃO LUIZ

www.teatrosaoluiz.egeac.pt
Everything from music to Shakespeare in a beautifully renovated theatre.
J8 Rua António Maria Cardoso 38 213 257 640 Baixa-Chiado 758; tram 28

MAINSTREAM CINEMA

The majority of big, first-release films are shown in multiplex cinemas in the many shopping malls around the city. The closest cinemas to the Baixa/Chiado area would be at the Centro Comercial Amoreiras.
F5 Avenida Eng. Duarte Pacheco 707 246 362 Marquês de Pombal 702, 711

TEATRO NACIONAL DONA MARIA II

www.teatro-dmaria.pt
There are two separate venues here hosting classical music and plays behind a classical façade.
K7 Praça Dom Pedro IV 213 250 835 or 213 250 800 Rossio 1, 2, 31, 36, 41, all Rossio services

TEATRO NACIONAL DE SÃO CARLOS

www.saocarlos.pt
Lisbon's premier opera house, which also hosts classical concerts, ballet and theatre, is a celebration of 18th-century rococo splendour.
J8 Largo de São Carlos 17–21 213 253 045 Box office: daily 1–7 Baixa-Chiado 758; tram 28

Restaurants

PRICES

Prices are approximate, based on a 3-course meal for one person.

€€€	over €25
€€	€15–€25
€	up to €15

BONJARDIM (€)

This Lisbon institution, with three outlets on the same street, appeals to all tastes. The downstairs dining room is lined with tiles and there are wooden beams upstairs. Also known as Rei dos Frangos after its specialty dish of grilled chicken.
J6 Travessa de Santo Antão 11–12 213 427 424 Daily lunch, dinner Restauradores

CAFÉ A BRASILEIRA (€)

The most famous of Lisbon's venerable coffeehouses at the heart of the fashionable Chiado district. A preferred retreat for writers and artists, notably the poet Fernando Pessoa, a statue of whom sits outside on the pavement. It has plenty of tables outdoors, and remains open until late, when the earlier refined atmosphere becomes less sedate.
J8 Rua Garrett 120 213 469 541 Daily 8am–2am Baixa-Chiado 758; tram 28E

CAFÉ MARTINHO DA ARCADA (€–€€)

Like the Nicola (▷ 37) on the Rossio and A Brasileira (▷ this page) in the Chiado, this old coffeehouse, founded in 1782, was a haunt of Lisbon's 19th-century literati. The adjoining restaurant is expensive, but the bar is still a good spot for coffee and snacks. Wood-panel counter.

K8 Praça do Comércio 3 218 879 259 Mon–Sat 7am–11pm Baixa-Chiado All services to Praça do Comércio; tram 15, 18, 25

CAFÉ NICOLA (€)

This lovely old place, dating from 1777, was a haunt for Lisbon's literary set in the 19th century and is now one of the city's most popular cafés.
K7 Rua Primeiro de Dezembro; entrance also at Praça Dom Pedro IV 24 213 460 579 Mon–Sat 8am–10pm, Sun 9–7 Rossio

CAFÉ NO CHIADO (€–€€)

www.cafenochiado.com
A restored 18th-century building filled with modern furnishings, serving worthy steak and chips to a young and artistic crowd.
J8 Largo do Picadeiro 10–12 213 460 501 Mon–Thu 10am–2am, Fri–Sat 10am–3am Baixa-Chiado 758; tram 28

CASA DO ALENTEJO (€€)

This restaurant, in a 19th-century Franco-Arabic-style building with wonderful tiles, is a celebration of the Alentejo region as much as of the Alentejan cuisine. There is often folk dancing on Saturday.
J6 Praça Santo Antão, Rua das Portas de Santo Antão 58 213 405 140 Daily lunch, dinner Restauradores

CASA CHINEZA (€)

Join locals for a mid-morning stand-up snack in this beautifully decorated traditional *pastelaria* in the heart of the Baixa.
K8 Rua da Aurea 274–78 213 423 680 Baixa-Chiado All Rossio services

CERVEJARIA PINÓQUIO (€)

Established in the Baixa for over 30 years, this is a simple, no-frills restaurant. Diners sit at long tables, service is quick and the fish fresh, brought in daily from Setúbal; if the sea is rough supplies run low.
J7 Praça dos Restauradores 79 213 465 106 Daily lunch, dinner Restauradores

CERVEJARIA TRINDADE (€–€€)

This large beer hall and *azulejo*-lined restaurant, in a former convent in the Chiado, is one of the city's oldest eating places, having been in business since 1836. The food is nothing special, but the place is a classic, and a fun spot.
J7 Rua Nova da Trindade 20c 213 423 506 Daily noon–1am Baixa-Chiado 758; tram 28

PASTELARIAS

If you are looking for a light meal in stylish surroundings, then it is worth considering traditional cafés and pastry shops such as Pastelaria Bénard (▷ 38), Café a Brasileira (▷ 36) and others. Best known as places for coffee and a pastry, they usually serve snacks and sandwiches too, and may stay open well into the evening.

CONFEITARIA NACIONAL (€)

www.confeitarianacional.com
Founded in 1829, the glass cases and painted panels bear witness to this stunning cake shop with 19th-century origins. It offers a plethora of tempting choices for anyone with a sweet tooth. The first floor serves lunches and afternoon tea, while the ground floor has a take-away service.
K7 Praça da Figueira 18B 213 424 470 Daily 8–8 Rossio All Rossio services; tram 12, 15

L'ENTRECOTE (€€)

The Chiado's smart set tend to make for this traditional, but relaxed wood-panelled dining room for the faultless presentation and fine, upmarket French-influenced food. Steaks, as the name suggests, are a specialty. There is a good two-course set menu daily.
J8 Rua do Alecrim 117 213 473 616 Daily lunch, dinner Baixa-Chiado 758; tram 28

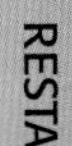

GAMBRINUS (€€€)
www.gambrinuslisboa.com
This restaurant, just off the Rossio, is one of Lisbon's most expensive. The culinary emphasis is on fish and seafood. The setting is suitably formal, with leather chairs and beamed ceiling. Reservations essential.
J6 25 Rua das Portas de Santo Antão 23 213 421 466 Daily lunch, dinner Restauradores

IBO (CAIS DA RIBEIRA) (€€–€€€)
In one of the many, now converted, warehouses along the dockside, this restaurant serves excellent fresh fish and seafood, and has fine views of the River Tagus.
J9 Armazem A-2, Cais do Sodré 213 423 611 Mon–Thu 12.30–3, 7–11; Fri–Sat 12.30–3, 7–1am Cais do Sodré 15, 18

PASTELARIA BÉNARD (€)
One of Lisbon's finest and long-established cafés and pastry shops; the desserts are particularly famous. On the Chiado's most fashionable street.
J8 Rua Garrett 104–106 213 473 133 Baixa-Chiado

PASTELARIA SUIÇA (€)
www.casasuica.pt
This café and pastry shop on Lisbon's main square competes with the historic Café Nicola (▷ 37) opposite. Both places have large and busy terraces.
K7 Praça Dom Pedro IV 96–104 213 214 090 Rossio

SOLMAR (€€)
In this big, busy, down-to-earth place in the Baxia district seafood is the focus but there are also game dishes on the menu. The dining room has a 1950s feel.
J6 Rua das Portas de Santo Antão 108 213 460 010 Daily lunch, dinner Restauradores All services to Avenida da Liberdade

TÁGIDE (€€€)
www.restaurantetagide.com
A very elegant restaurant up from the waterfront on a hilltop in the Chiado district. Tiled portraits of Portuguese queens punctuate the white-washed walls, and chandeliers hang above. Book early to secure a window table with lovely views over the port and city. Specialties include stuffed crab and cold orange and lemon soufflé with hot chocolate sauce.
J8 Largo Académia Nacional de Belas Artes 18–20 213 404 010 Tue–Sat 12.30–7, Fri 12.30–12 Baixa-Chiado 758; tram 15, 28

TASCAS

Portugal's traditional eating haunts are known as *tascas,* from the old word *tascar*, to eat. A *tasca* serves no-frills cuisine—good honest traditional fare based on old 'poormans' recipes that used bread, pork bits and whatever the earth provided. Portions are huge and prices very reasonable. This food is known as *comida regional,* though not relating to any particular region but rather to the country as a whole. It's the same as *comida típica*.

TAVARES (€€€)
www.tavaresrico.pt
For years this glittering old-world establishment, founded as a café in 1784, had a reputation as the best of Lisbon's grand restaurants. It still attracts politicians, diplomats and the literary set.
J8 Rua da Misericórdia 35 213 421 112 Tue–Sat lunch, dinner Baixa-Chiado Tram 15, 28

TERREIRO DO PAÇO (€€€)
www.terreiropaco.com
This stylish spot has won plaudits from around the world as one of Europe's best restaurants. Modern takes on Portuguese food served in a brick-vaulted room. Near the Lisboa Welcome Centre.
K8 Praça do Comércio 210 312 850 Mon–Fri lunch, dinner; Sat dinner only Terréiro do Paço/Baixa-Chiado All bus services to Praça do Comércio

This is the oldest part of the city, where a labyrinth of steep, narrow streets crammed with shops, restaurants and bars, Moorish architecture and splendid churches is watched over by a castle on the hill.

Sights	**42–51**
Walk	**52**
Shopping	**53**
Entertainment and Nightlife	**53**
Restaurants	**54**

Top 25 TOP 25

Alfama ▷ **42**
Campo de Santa Clara ▷ **44**
Museu das Artes Decorativas ▷ **45**
Castelo de São Jorge ▷ **46**
Sé ▷ **48**

5
6
7
8
9
Hospital do Desterro
Rua Nova do Desterro
R Desterro
RUA DA PALMA
Rua do Benformoso
Rua da Bombarda
Martim Moniz
Rua M P de Lima
MOURARI
Costa do Castelo
Castelo de São Jorge
Rua de São Mam
Santo António de Lisboa
Nossa Senhora Conceição Velha
RUA
0
250 m
0
250 yds
H
J
K

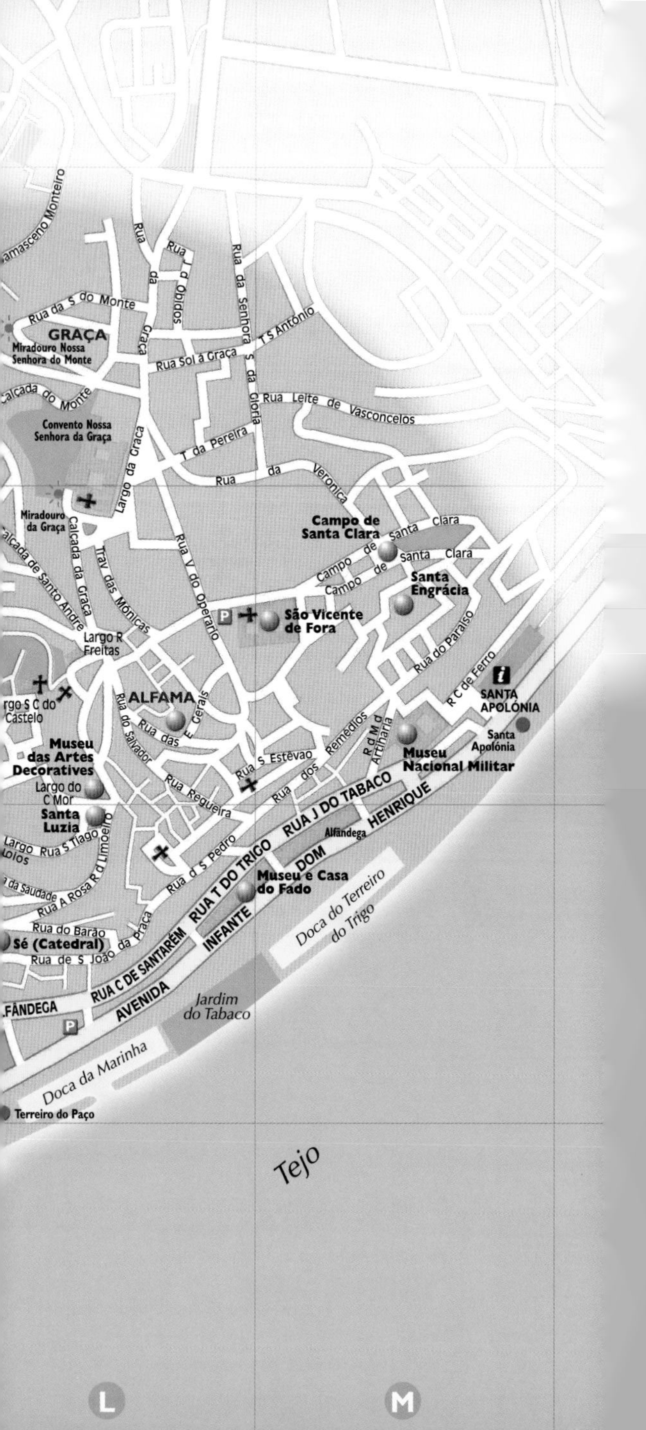

GRAÇA
Miradouro Nossa Senhora do Monte
Convento Nossa Senhora da Graça
Miradouro da Graça
Rua da S do Monte
Rua Sol à Graça
T S António
Rua Leite de Vasconcelos
T da Pereira
Rua da Veronica
Largo da Graça
Calcada da Graça
Trav das Mónicas
Rua V do Operario
Calcada de Santo Andre
Largo R Freitas
Campo de Santa Clara
Santa Engrácia
São Vicente de Fora
Rua do Paraiso
R C de Ferro
SANTA APOLÓNIA
Santa Apolónia
ALFAMA
Museu das Artes Decoratives
Largo do C Mor
Santa Luzia
Rua do Salvador
Rua das E Gerais
Rua S Estêvao
Rua dos Remedios
Rua Regueira
Museu Nacional Militar
RUA J DO TABACO
Alfândega
DOM HENRIQUE
Museu e Casa do Fado
RUA T DO TRIGO
INFANTE
Doca do Terreiro do Trigo
Rua d S Pedro
Rua S Tiago
R d Limoeiro
Rua A Rosa
Rua do Barão
Sé (Catedral)
Rua de S João da Praça
RUA C DE SANTARÉM
AVENIDA
Jardim do Tabaco
Doca da Marinha
Terreiro do Paço
Tejo
L
M

Alfama

TOP 25

HIGHLIGHTS

- Castelo de São Jorge (▷ 46)
- Church of São Miguel
- Church of Santo Estevão
- Church of Santa Luzia (▷ 51)
- Pátio das Flores
- Largo das Portas do Sol
- Miradouro de Santa Luzia

TIPS

- If you do get lost, go downhill and you will get your bearings.
- Be aware of pickpockets.

This warren of atmospheric old streets is tailor-made for random exploration. The narrow alleys, hanging washing, flower-laden windows and beautifully preserved tile-fronted mansions are like an image from the past.

Springs Of all Lisbon's old quarters, none is more evocative or pleasant to explore than the Alfama, a labyrinth of timeless vignettes and Medina-like streets that still have an Arabic feel. The area takes its name from a Moorish word, *alhama*, or fountain, a reference to the hot springs in Largo das Alcaçarías. As a distinct enclave, however, it is much older, probably dating back to the first Phoenician or Roman traders who settled in the area around the present-day Castelo. Between 711 and 1147 it became an important Moorish suburb,

Only the cars give away the fact that this is Lisbon in the 21st century (left); intricate azelujos *(tiles) decorate a house in the Alfama district (middle); on the tourist trail in the narrow streets (right); among the rooftops in old Lisbon (below left); fish for sale in the Rua de São Pedro (below right)*

and later the home of the city's first churches. In time it became a retreat for the city's élite, losing its cachet only after the 1755 earthquake.

Sights Today for the most part the area is a robust and old-fashioned residential district, though the restorers, gentrifying many of the once humble dwellings, the restaurants and the trendy shops are beginning to take the edge off its pristine appeal. The best way to see the district is to wander at random amid the streets and half-hidden squares—maps are almost useless here. Streets you might try to head for include Rua de São Pedro, Rua São Miguel, Beco de Cardosa, the Pátio das Flores, Largo de São Rafael and Rua dos Remédios. Try also to take in the viewpoints at Largo das Portas do Sol and the Miradouro de Santa Luzia, which has several good cafés.

THE BASICS

L7/8–M8
Around Castelo de São Jorge
Cafés, bars and restaurants
37; tram 12, 28
Poor
Avoid the area after dark

Campo de Santa Clara

The perfect pitch—flea markets in the shadow of Santa Engrácia in Campo de Santa Clara

THE BASICS

M7
Campo de Santa Clara
Feira da Ladra: Tue 7–1, Sat 7–4
Cafés
12, 34; tram 28
Poor
Watch for pickpockets

HIGHLIGHTS

- Feira da Ladra
- Santa Engrácia
- São Vicente de Fora
- Jardim Boto Machado
- Miradouro da Senhora do Monte

Campo de Santa Clara deserves a special mention for its churches, but it should preferably be visited on a market day, when stalls are set up by individuals selling anything from old postcards to used car batteries.

Lively market Campo de Santa Clara lies on the eastern margins of the Alfama district, one of Lisbon's most atmospheric quarters. The square and its surrounding streets are best known for their flea market, the Feira da Ladra (the 'Thieves' Market'), which takes place here on Tuesday morning and all day Saturday. The Feira's covered stalls (in the middle of the square) sell a predictable assortment of market goods—food, shoes, cheap clothes and household items—while the peripheral stalls deal in books, old postcards and miscellaneous bric-a-brac. Don't be fooled; genuine bargains are hard to find, but you can spend an enjoyable morning browsing here. There is another market nearby, Mercado Municipal de Santa Clara (▷ 53).

Vistas Market or not, the area around Campo de Santa Clara would still be worth exploring. Two of the city's more interesting churches are nearby: Santa Engrácia (▷ 50) to the southeast and São Vicente de Fora (▷ 51) to the northwest, the former completed only in 1966, the latter in 1704. São Vicente is the burial place of many of Portugal's kings and queens. At the heart of the square itself is the Jardim Boto Machado, a garden full of palms and exotic plants, with a fine view.

Stunning displays of antiques and furniture in the elegant Museu das Artes Decorativas

Museu das Artes Decorativas

This beautifully restored 17th-century palace has a stunning collection of furniture, carpets and antiques displayed in a period setting, giving the visitor a picture of upper-class Lisbon life in the 18th and 19th centuries.

Bequest Lisbon's beguiling Museum of the Decorative Arts is housed in the 17th-century palace of the Counts of Azurara, former home of Ricardo do Espírito Santo Silva (1900–55), a Portuguese philanthropist. He left the house and his private collection of art and objects to the nation in 1953. Both house and collection, run by the Espírito Santo Silva Foundation, are now open to the public. The foundation also supports a series of workshops (next door) in which you can watch people practising traditional skills such as bookbinding, wood-carving and cabinet-making.

Exquisite home Espírito Santo had exceptional taste, with the result that his collection embraces some of the finest examples of Portuguese and other art and objects. The palace itself is beautiful, with its original 17th-century wooden floors, painted ceilings and panels of blue and white *azulejos* (tiles). This forms the perfect setting for the lovely furniture, antiques, tapestries, porcelain, ceramics and rugs from Arraiolos (a central Portuguese town renowned for its exquisite carpets). Perhaps the most captivating areas are the bedrooms, complete with tiny four-poster beds, and the upstairs dining room, with its grandfather clock and fine painted ceiling.

THE BASICS

www.fress.pt
L7
Largo das Portas do Sol 2
218 881 991
Daily 10–5. Closed public hols
Café
37; tram 12, 28
Very poor: many stairs
Moderate

HIGHLIGHTS

- Palace
- Furniture
- Carpets
- Painted ceilings
- Bedrooms
- Tapestries
- Silverware
- Inlaid chess table

Castelo de São Jorge

Perched high on a hill, the castle dominates the city and offers terrific views

THE BASICS

www.castelosaojorge.egac.pt
L7
Rua Costa do Castelo
218 800 620
Castle and Olisipónia: Nov–end Feb daily 9–5.30; Mar–end Oct 9–8.30
Câmara Escura: Daily 10–5 (weather permitting)
Restaurant and café
37; tram 12, 28
Poor
Moderate (includes Olisipónia and Câmara Escura)

HIGHLIGHTS

- Views
- Gardens
- Battlements and towers
- Olisípónia multimedia show
- Parade ground

Lisbon's ancient fortress, with its breathtaking views and lovely gardens, is a shady oasis where you can retreat from the challenges of sightseeing to enjoy some peace and quiet.

Defence Lisbon's evocative castle marks the city's birthplace, the spot where Phoenician traders probably first made camp, attracted by the area's natural port, its easily defended position and the agricultural potential. Later it was fortified by the Romans, Visigoths and Moors, the defeat of the last, at the hands of Afonso Henriques in 1147, marking a turning point in the campaign to oust the Moors from Portugal. Henriques took the fortress after a 17-week siege, a victory tainted by the actions of his British and French allies—supposedly Christian Crusaders—who ran amok, pillaging and murdering Moors and Christians alike.

Views Today the castle's walls have been rather over-restored. Its pristine stonework makes it hard to believe that much of the 12th-century original remains, though its lofty site and beautiful grounds are irresistible. The outer walls enclose the little district of Santa Cruz, one of the medieval jewels of the old Alfama district. A statue of Afonso Henriques glowers over the main entrance, beyond which lies a lovely array of verdant terraces and leafy walkways, and ducks and swans glide across limpid pools. Inside the castle is Olisipónia, an interpretive and multimedia venue. Best of all, however, are the superlative views over the rooftops from the old Moorish battlements.

Sé

TOP 25

HIGHLIGHTS

- Twin towers
- Rose window
- Baptismal font
- Bartolomeu Chapel (1324)
- *Nativity*, Joaquim Machado de Castro (1766)
- Tomb of Lopo Fernandes Pacheco
- Cloister
- Treasury
- Reliquary of St. Vincent
- Dom José I monstrance

Nothing evokes a stronger sense of Lisbon's long history than views of the formidable cathedral, whose ancient stone towers can be seen above the rooftops from the Baixa and the view-points of the Bairro Alto.

History Lisbon's cathedral was begun around 1150, soon after Afonso Henriques, Portugal's first king, had captured the city from the Moors. It was the city's first church, and legend claims it stands on the site of a mosque. Like other Portuguese cathedrals of similar vintage—Évora, Porto, Coimbra—it has a fortress-like appearance, the result of its plain Romanesque design and the tumultuous times in which it was built, when there was still a threat from the Moors. Much of its original shell survives, notably its distinctive squat

Take a tram up to the impressive cathedral, in the Alfama district of the city (left); the soaring arches create an awe-inspiring sense of grandeur (right)

towers, which unlike the old chancel withstood the earthquakes of 1344 and 1755, as well as the attentions of restorers.

Interior On the left as you enter the church is a font, reputedly used in 1195 to baptize St. Antony of Padua, who was born in Lisbon. The first chapel on the left is decorated with an intricately carved Nativity scene, the work of 18th-century sculptor Joaquim Machado de Castro. More beautiful still is the tomb of Lopo Fernandes Pacheco, a courtier of Afonso IV, in the chapel on the right of the Gothic ambulatory. The ruined 13th-century Gothic cloister is worth seeing for its lovely sculptural fragments. According to legend, over the years the church has been protected by ravens brought here by Afonso in 1173, until the last of the descendants died recently.

THE BASICS

www.ippar.pt
L8
Largo da Sé
218 876 628
Cathedral: Mon–Sat 9–7, Sun 9–5. Cloister: daily 10–5
Terréiso do Paço
37; tram 12, 28
Poor
Cathedral: free. Cloister: inexpensive

More to See

MUSEU E CASA DO FADO

www.museudofado.egeac.pt

An intriguing museum that illustrates this Portuguese passion. Learn about the history, hear the music, see how the 10-stringed Portuguese guitars are made and visit a 1940s *fado* house.

L8 Largo do Chafariz de Dentro 1 218 823 470 Tue–Sun 10–6 (last entry 5.30) Café 28, 35, 39, 90, 107, 208 Inexpensive

MUSEU NACIONAL MILITAR

www.geira-pt/mmilitar

Following a fire and the 1755 earthquake, the complex was rebuilt as an arsenal, becoming the Artillery Museum in 1851. As well as an artillery collection—one of the world's best—the museum has extensive displays of guns, pistols and swords. Among them are Portuguese pieces from the 16th century, and objects of French, Dutch, English, Spanish and Arab origin.

M7 Largo do Museu da Artilharia 218 842 569 Tue–Sun 2–5 Santa Apolónia 28, 35, 745, 759, 794 Inexpensive

NOSSA SENHORA DA CONCEIÇAO VELHA

Like Santa Luzia, this is one to enjoy from the outside. Most of the church collapsed in 1755, but the south doorway survived as a fine and rare example of the Manueline style—the ornate form of Gothic associated with the reign of Manuel I (1495–1521), when wealth poured into Portugal.

K8 Rua da Alfândega 37; tram 18, 25

SANTA ENGRÁCIA

This large baroque building, begun in 1682, survived the 1755 earthquake but was not completed until 1966, when the cupola was finally added. The fact that this project took 284 years to complete has led to a little Portuguese idiom—*obras de Santa Engrácia*—used as a synonym for delayed or unfinished work. The early design focuses on a balanced Greek Cross with four towers and curving arms, and was influenced by new departures in Italian baroque architecture of the period. The result is a slightly

One for military buffs, the Museu Nacional Militar

chilled and over-precise building, well suited to its memorial function.

M7 Campo de Santa Clara 218 854 820 Tue–Sun 10–5 12, 34; tram 28 Inexpensive. Free Sun

SANTA LUZIA

The reason to visit this modest church is obvious from the outside. Its exterior walls are covered in *azulejos* depicting Lisbon before and after the earthquake of 1755, and its garden is laid out as a charming viewpoint, the Miradouro de Santa Luzia.

L8 Largo de Santa Luzia 37; tram 28

SANTO ANTÓNIO DE LISBOA

This little church stands on the site of the house where St. Antony was born in 1195. Built after the 1755 earthquake, it contains paintings by Pedro de Carvalho, who was responsible for the decoration of many churches after the disaster. The square in which the church sits is called Santo António de Sé because the church is immediately in front of the cathedral. A small museum displays objects related to the saint's life.

L8 Largo de Santo António de Sé 24 Museum: 218 860 447 Church: daily 8–7.30. Museum: Tue–Sun 10–1, 2–6. Closed public hols 37; tram 28 Church: free. Museum: inexpensive

SÃO VICENTE DE FORA

São Vicente was built between 1582 and 1627, over the site of a 12th-century church erected to commemorate the Crusaders' victory over the Moors. The construction of the present church took place during Portugal's period of subjugation to the Spanish, and was the work of Philip II of Spain's principal architect, the Italian Filippo Terzi. His cupola was felled by the 1755 earthquake and has been replaced by a more modest dome, though the majestic nave survives, with its glorious coffered vault and extravagant baroque altar.

M7 Largo de São Vicente 218 824 400 Tue–Sat 9–5, Sun 9–12.30 12, 37; tram 28 Church: free. Monastery: moderate

Detail of the baroque-inspired dome of the church of Santa Engrácia

Around the Alfama

The best way to explore the Alfama district, with its maze of tiny streets, is on foot. Here you will really experience old Lisbon.

DISTANCE: 2.5km (1.5 miles) **ALLOW:** 2 hours

START

SÉ (CATHEDRAL)

L8 Terreiro do Paço 37; tram 12, 28

❶ Make your way to Lisbon's striking cathedral, the Sé (▷ 48–49). Keeping the cathedral to your right, walk uphill along Rua da Augusta da Rosa. Continue to Miradouro de Santa Luzia.

❷ Pause at the splendid viewpoint. Cross the road to visit the Museu das Artes Decorativas (▷ 45). As you leave the museum, turn right (back the way you came).

❸ Take the first right, Travessa de Santa Luzia, and continue uphill (bearing right) following the yellow signs to the Castelo de São Jorge (▷ 46).

❹ Walk the length of the walkway under the castle walls, emerging through a green iron gate into Largo do Menino de Deus (down to your left). Turn left into the shabby square.

❺ Find Rua de Santa Marinha at the top (north) side of this square.

❻ Follow this road to São Vicente de Fora church (▷ 51). Take the street to the left of the church into Campo de Santa Clara (▷ 44).

❼ Walk to the small garden, then drop right to come around behind the church of Santa Engrácia (▷ 50). With your back to the façade, go left past the brown-tiled house ahead. Turn right onto Rua dos Remédios at the bottom. Detour south to visit the Museu Nacional Militar (▷ 50) or turn right onto Rua São Estêvão.

❽ Turn left on to the atmospheric Rua de São Miguel. From here you can return to the cathedral and make your way back to the Metro.

SÉ (CATHEDRAL)

END

Shopping

ADIVINHO
www.adivinho.com
This large wine cellar sells port wines and wines of every Portuguese vineyard. Have a free tasting while you watch the vineyard presentation.
K8 Travessa do Almada 24 218 860 419 37; tram 28

FÁBRICA DE CÉRAMICA VIÚVA LAMEGO
www.viuvalamego.com
This factory dates back to 1879. The factory shop is adorned with tiles on its exterior, and sells mainly copies of traditional designs, together with a small selection of pottery. It will also design and make tiles to order.
K5 Largo do Intendente 25 218 852 408 Intendente 708, 40; tram 28

MERCADO MUNICIPAL DE SANTA CLARA
A vibrant food market, particularly good if you are going on a picnic.
M7 Campo de Santo Clara 12, 34; tram 28

M. MURTEIRA
www.murteira-antiguidades.com
If walking up to the Castelo de Sâo Jorge you will pass this charming antiques shop, with curiosities from the 18th–19th century. Everything from bed heads to bird cages.
L8 Rua Augusta Rosa 19–21 218 863 851 37; tram 28

Entertainment and Nightlife

CLUBE DE FADO
www.clube-de-fado.com
A great venue popular with tourists, which puts on quality *fado* performances in a colonnaded arched hall.
L8 Rua São João da Praça 94 218 852 704 Daily 8pm–2am 37; tram 12, 28

LUX
www.luxfragil.com
Over two floors in a riverside warehouse, with a cool retro interior. DJs play a mix of dance and mainstream music to a stylish crowd. When the noise gets too much, chill-out on the terrace.
M7 Avenida Infante D. Henrique, Armazém A, Cais da Pedra, Santa Apolónia 218 820 890 Tue–Sat 10pm–6am 28, 35, 745, 759, 794

ONDA JAZZ
www.ondajazz.com
Head down toward the waterfront to this cosy bar that hosts live bands playing jazz, bossa nova, world music and other popular sounds.
L8 Arco de Jesus 7 218 873 064 28, 35, 745, 759, 794

HISTORY OF *FADO*

Lisbon and Coimbra are the two great cities of *fado*—a melancholy form of traditional singing accompanied by guitar. Passion, fate and regrets are the main themes. It may originate from African slave songs, or have Moorish roots. In Lisbon, the singer (*fadista*) is nearly always a woman, and is accompanied by one or two impassive male guitarists. *Coimbra fado* is sung by men, and has a less heart-rending quality.

PARREIRINHA DE ALFAMA
Another of the city's more venerable clubs, with some of the greatest names in *fado*. Both the cover charge and food prices are lower than those of its rivals. No dancing.
M8 Beco do Espírito Santo 1, off Largo do Chafariz de Dentro 218 868 209 Daily 8pm–2am 37; tram 28

Restaurants

PRICES

Prices are approximate, based on a 3-course meal for one person.

€€€ over €25
€€ €15–€25
€ under €15

BICA DO SAPATO (€€–€€€)

www.bicadosapato.com

Bica do Sapato is one of Lisbon's trendiest restaurants. It has a modern interior of wood, glass and chrome, views over the river, and excellent sushi.

M8 Avenida Infante D. Henrique, Armazém B, Cais da Pedra, Santa Apolónia 218 810 320 Tue–Sun lunch, dinner, Mon dinner only. Sushi bar Mon–Sat dinner only 28, 35, 745, 759, 794

CAFÉ CERCA MOURA (€)

Close to the Miradouro de Santa Luzia in Largo das Portas do Sol, this café has fine views of the River Tejo and a good selection of snacks and drinks.

L8 Largo das Portas do Sol 4 218 874 859 Daily noon–2am 37; tram 12E, 28E

CASANOVA (€€)

www.restaurantecasanostra.com

This restaurant offers good-value Italian food with a fun atmosphere—diners attract the waiter by turning on the red light above the table. Opt for pizza cooked fresh in the wood-fired oven, or for a more hearty meal try a slow-cooked bean dish. No reservations, but you shouldn't have to wait long for a place at the shared tables.

M8 Av. Infante D. Henrique, Cais da Pedra, Armazém 7 Loja B 218 877 532 Tue–Sun 12.30–1am 28, 35, 745, 759, 794

DELHI PALACE (€€)

A popular, Indian-owned restaurant west of the cathedral that offers a mixture of Indian and Italian food, though it is recommended more for its curries than its pasta.

L8 Rua da Padaria 18–20 218 884 203 Tue–Sun lunch, dinner Terréiro do Paço 37; tram 12, 28

FAZ FIGURA (€€€)

www.fazfigura.com

This restaurant provides excellent service and fine views over the River Tagus. The best on the menu includes *feijoada de marisco* (shellfish) and seafood *cataplana* (a large round-bottomed copper dish).

M7 Rua do Paraíso 15B 218 868 981 Daily lunch and dinner 34, 35

HALF PORTIONS

Servings tend to be generous in Portugal, and many soups and starters are rich and filling enough to be meals in themselves. If you can't manage whole portions, ask if you can have a half portion, or share one serving between two—many restaurants are happy to serve smaller portions, especially those in the lower price range, and some even list half portions on the menu.

LAUTASCO (€€)

This Alfama restaurant is popular with locals and visitors, who come here not so much for the simple Portuguese fare but for the delightful atmospheric courtyard.

L8 Beco do Azinhal 7A, off Rua de São Pedro-Largo Chafariz de Dentro 218 860 173 Mon–Sat lunch, dinner 28, 35, 745, 759, 794

MALMEQUER BEMMEQUER (€–€€)

A welcoming choice in an evocative street in the Alfama district. Plenty of basic Portuguese dishes.

L8 Rua São Miguel 23–25, Largo de São Miguel 218 876 535 Wed–Sun lunch, dinner, Tue dinner only 37; tram 28

VIA GRAÇA (€€€)

www.restauranteviagraca.com

A romantic spot on a hillside in Graça, with panoramic views of the city. Big portions of classic Portuguese cuisine are enhanced by a subtle combination of tastes.

L6 Rua Damasceno Monteiro 9-B 218 870 830 Mon–Fri lunch, dinner, Sat–Sun dinner Tram 28

Bairro Alto/The West

Bairro Alto stands high above the city, a bohemian area with a vibrant nightlife. On the western slopes lie Estrela, crowned by its basilica, prosperous São Bento and Lapa, which runs into Santos and the Alcântara.

Sights	**58–64**
Tour	**65**
Shopping	**66**
Entertainment and Nightlife	**67–68**
Restaurants	**69–72**

Top 25 — TOP 25

Bairro Alto ▷ **58**
Basílica da Estrela ▷ **59**
Igreja de São Roque ▷ **60**
Museu Nacional de Arte Antiga ▷ **62**

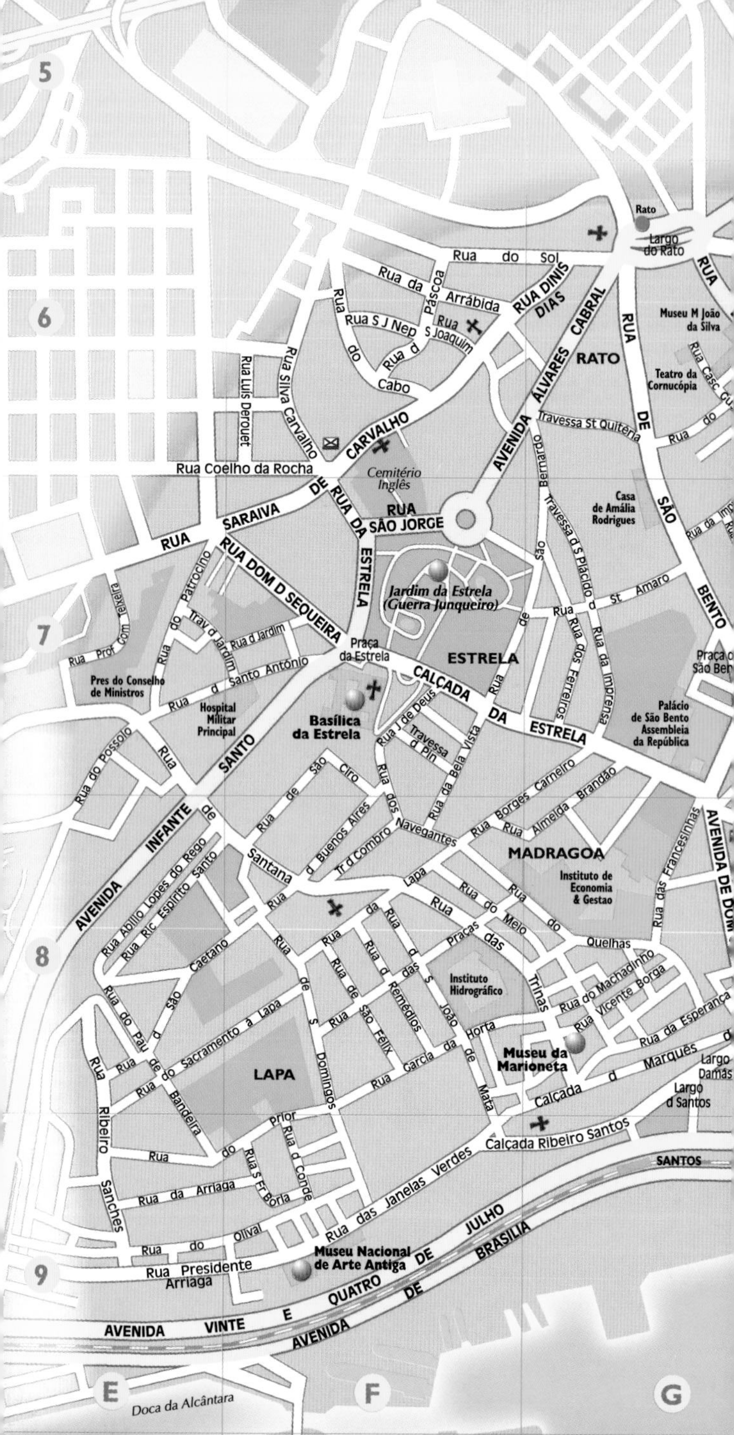
5
6
7
8
9
E
F
G
Rato
Largo do Rato
Rua do Sol
Rua da Arrábida
Rua da Páscoa
Rua Dinis Dias
Rua S J Nep
Rua S Joaquim
Rua do Cabo
Rua d
Rua Silva Carvalho
Rua Luís Derouet
Rua Coelho da Rocha
Rua Saraiva de Carvalho
Avenida Álvares Cabral
Rua de São Bento
Museu M João da Silva
Rato
Teatro da Cornucópia
Rua do
Travessa St Quitéria
Cemitério Inglês
Rua São Jorge
Rua da Estrela
Rua São Bernardo
Travessa d S Plácido
Casa de Amália Rodrigues
Rua Dom D Sequeira
Rua do Patrocínio
Trav d Jardim
Rua d Jardim
Rua Prof Com Teixeira
Jardim da Estrela (Guerra Junqueiro)
Rua d St Amaro
Rua de
Rua dos Ferreiros
Rua da Imprensa
Praça de São Bento
Praça da Estrela
Estrela
Calçada da Estrela
Pres do Conselho de Ministros
Rua d Santo António
Hospital Militar Principal
Basílica da Estrela
Rua J de Deus
Travessa d Pin
Rua da Bela Vista
Palácio de São Bento Assembleia da República
Rua do Possolo
Rua Santo
Rua de São Ciro
Rua dos Navegantes
Rua Borges Carneiro
Rua Almeida Brandão
Avenida de Dom
Avenida Infante de Santana
Rua de Buenos Aires
Tr d Combro
Lapa
Madragoa
Instituto de Economia & Gestao
Rua das Francesinhas
Rua Abílio Lopes do Rego
Rua Ric Espírito Santo
Rua do Meio
Rua das Praças
Rua das Trinas
Rua do Quelhas
Rua da Lapa
Rua de São Caetano
Rua d Remédios
Rua de S Domingos
Rua de São Félix
Rua de S João de Mata
Instituto Hidrográfico
Rua do Machadinho
Rua Vicente Borga
Rua da Esperança
Rua do Pau de Bandeira
Rua do Sacramento à Lapa
Rua Garcia da Horta
Museu da Marioneta
Calçada d Marquês
Largo Damas
Largo d Santos
Lapa
Rua Ribeiro Sanches
Rua do Prior
Rua d Conde
Rua S Fr Borla
Calçada Ribeiro Santos
Santos
Rua da Arriaga
Rua das Janelas Verdes
Rua do Olival
Museu Nacional de Arte Antiga
Rua Presidente Arriaga
Avenida Vinte e Quatro de Julho
Avenida de Brasília
Doca da Alcântara

Rua do Vale do Pereiro
Rua Barata Salgueiro
RUA DO SALITRE
Rua N São Mamede
Teatros
Museu Zoológico e Antropológico
Jardim Botânico
ESCOLA POLITÉCNICA
Universidade Internacional
Praça da Alegria
Rua Mãe de Água
Rua St António Glória
Rua da Glória
Rua das Taipas
Matos Sequeira
Rua d Mte Oliv
Rua M Portugal
Marçal
Rua Cec d Sousa
Praça do Príncipe Real
RUA DOM PEDRO V
Palmeiras
Rua d Jasm
Rua de S
Manuel Bernardes
Piedade
Rua das
Rua Eduardo Coelho
Trav Palm
Travessa C Soure
Miradouro de São Pedro de Alcântara
Elevador da Glória
C da Glória
RUA S PALCÂNTARA
Museu de Arte Sacra
Rua Nova do Loureiro
Rua d Vinha
Travessa da Boa Hora
Rua do Século
Trav St Ter
Rua da Quintinha
Rua dos Polais
Rua Academia Ciências
Academia das Ciências de Lisboa
Igreja de São Roque
Travessa da Queimada
Rua da Rosa
Rua da Luz
RUA D MISERICÓRDIA
Trav de Arrochela
Rua d Cruz
Rua d Vale
BAIRRO ALTO
Travessa dos Fiéis de Deus
Rua das Gáveas
S Catarina
Jos
Calçada do Combro
Rua d P de São Bento
Rua d Loreto
Praça L de Camões
Poço d Negros
Rua d Sol
Tr do Alcaide
Rua de Sta Catarina
R d H Seca
Rua d Poço
Rua Tomás Fernandes
Rua d Almada
Rua da Bica D B
Elevador da Bica
Rua das Chagas
Rua da Emenda
Rua d Flores
ALECRIM
Rua da Boa Vista
Abrantes
Boq do Duro
Rua Inst Industrial
Rua dos Ferreiros
Rua d S Paulo
Central Telefónica
Rua de Dom Luis I
Rua d Ribeira
Rua Nova do Carvalho
RUA DO
Boa dos
Praça de Dom Luís I
Cais do Sodré
Praça D da Terceira
AVENIDA VINTE E QUATRO DE JULHO
AVENIDA DE BRASILIA
CAIS DO SODRÉ
Cais do Sodré
Tejo
0
250 m
0
250 yds
H
J

Bairro Alto

After dark the sound of fado fills the air (left); a typical street in the Bairro Alto (right)

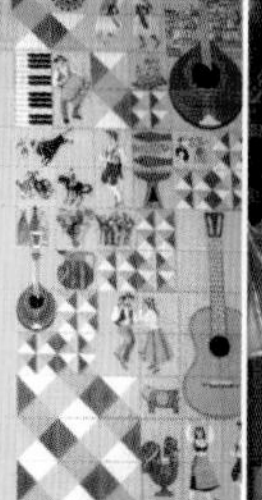

THE BASICS

H7–H8

Streets enclosed by Rua da Boa Vista, Rua da Misericórdia, Rua do Século and Rua Dom Pedro V

Many bars and cafés

Baixa-Chiado or Restauradores/Elevador da Glória

Tram 28

Very poor

HIGHLIGHTS

- Elevador da Glória
- Solar do Vinho do Porto
- Miradouro de São Pedro de Alcântara
- Rua de Atalaia (shopping)
- Rua do Diário de Notícías (shopping)

Traditionally the bohemian haunt of students, artists and writers, the narrow cobbled streets of the Bairro Alto, home of the traditional *fado* singing, should not be missed on any visit to the city.

Nightlife The Bairro Alto, or Upper Town, is one of Lisbon's liveliest and most distinctive quarters, and one of the five loosely defined areas that make up the heart of the old city. Traditionally a working-class area, it was first developed in the 1500s, when merchants settled here. It was hardly damaged by the 1755 earthquake, and rises in a close-knit grid of 16th-century streets up the very steep slopes west of the Chiado and Baixa districts. During the day its quiet corners are filled with the sort of evocative scenes you find all over Lisbon—washing strung from the windows and children playing in the streets. As night falls, by contrast, the restaurants and bars open and by 10pm the strains of *fado* can be heard as the area becomes the principal focus of Lisbon's nightlife.

Sights Exploring the Bairro's streets is an activity worth pursuing for its own sake, but some sights deserve special attention. These include the Elevador da Glória, a funicular built in 1885, which will save you a lot of climbing by carrying you up from the Baixa district below. Other sights are the Solar do Vinho do Porto, run by the Port Wine Institute, and the Igreja de São Roque (▷ 60–61). The Miradouro de São Pedro de Alcântara (▷ 64) has some fine views over the city.

The austere Basílica da Estrela holds some superb treasures within its walls

Basílica da Estrela

The austerity of neoclassical architecture is not to everyone's taste, but it is difficult to remain unaffected by the sheer scale of the Estrela basilica—not to mention the sweeping views from its dome.

Offering Like the Palácio de Fronteira, the Basílica da Estrela lies some way from the heart of the city—2km (1.2 miles) to the west of the Bairro Alto—but it is more than worth the effort required to see it. You will be doubly rewarded if you combine a trip here with a visit to the Jardim da Estrela (Jardim Guerra Junqueiro), one of the city's most beautiful gardens (▷ 64). The basilica, a monumental white edifice, was founded by Dona Maria I in 1779 as a votive offering for the birth of a son. It is a neoclassical masterpiece.

Impressive The church's architects, Mateus Vicente and Reinaldo Manuel, were influenced by the convent at Mafra (▷ 106), a building whose main attribute is size. Size is also the basilica's defining feature, the austere interior a cavernous expanse of marble. To the left of the high altar lies the tomb of Dona Maria I, who died in Brazil in 1816 and whose body was returned to Portugal for burial six years later. Unlike male scions of the Bragança royal dynasty, who were embalmed for posterity, Maria was simply adorned with herbs and enclosed in three tight-closing coffins, one inside the other. It is said that when these were opened to transfer the body back to Portugal, two ladies-in-waiting assisting in the ceremony fainted at the stench from the putrefied corpse.

THE BASICS

- F7
- Largo da Estrela
- 213 960 915
- Daily 8–7
- Rato
- 713, 773; tram 25, 28
- Poor
- Free

HIGHLIGHTS

- Façade
- Twin towers
- Tomb of Dona Maria I
- Views from the dome
- Jardim da Estrela

Igreja de São Roque

HIGHLIGHTS

- Painted wooden ceiling
- Capela de São Roque
- Tile decoration
- Capela de São João Baptista
- Mosaics

TIP

- Beside the church is the Museu de Arte Sacra, with a rich collection of paintings, embroidery and ecclesiastical plates.

Asked to highlight the most extravagant piece of decorative folly in Lisbon, you would have to suggest the Igreja de São Roque, and in particular its chapels, which groan under the weight of gold, gilt, marble and other precious materials.

Lavish interior Little in the plain façade of this church prepares you for the decorative glory within. Commissioned by the Jesuits in the 16th century, the building, of 1565, was the work of Filippo Terzi, also responsible for the church of São Vicente across the city. His original façade fell victim to the 1755 earthquake, but not the interior, which was saved, according to popular belief, by the personal intervention of St. Roch (São Roque). Inside, the *trompe l'œil* painting on the ceiling is a triumph, while each of the eight chapels lining the

The magnificently decorated interior of the Church of São Roque, built in the 16th century following Filippo Terzi's plans, displays a wealth of riches and adornments

nave is a decorative masterpiece. The third chapel on the right, the Capela de São Roque, has some of the finest *azulejos* (tiles) in the city; for example the work of Francisco de Matos in 1584, his only known commission.

Chapel The fourth chapel on the left, the Capela de São João Baptista, though less immediately impressive, has been called the most expensive chapel for its size ever built. Commissioned in 1742 by João V, it was designed by Vanvitelli, the papal architect, and built in Rome. There it was blessed by Pope Benedict XIV before being shipped to Lisbon, where its ensemble of precious materials—ivory, amethyst, porphyry and Carrara marble among others—was reassembled. Note the chapel's 'paintings', which are not paintings but extraordinarily detailed mosaics.

THE BASICS

- J7
- Largo Trindade Coelho
- 213 235 000; museum 213 235 380
- Museum: Tue–Wed, Fri–Sun 10–6; Thu 2–9. Closed public hols. Church: daily 8.30–5
- Baixa-Chiado
- 758; Elevador da Glória
- Poor
- Church: free. Museum: inexpensive; free on Sun and public hols

Museu Nacional de Arte Antiga

HIGHLIGHTS

- *Adoration of St. Vincent*, Nuno Gonçalves
- Cook Triptych, Grão Vasco
- *Annunciation*, Frei Carlos
- *Temptation of St. Antony*, Hieronymus Bosch
- *Madonna and Child*, Memling
- *St. Jerome*, Albrecht Dürer
- St. Augustine, Piero della Francesca

TIPS

- Pick up a leaflet to aid your visit.
- Take a lunch break in the pleasant café.

Lisbon may have few internationally acclaimed galleries, but in this wonderful museum, as well as the Gulbenkian Museum (▷ 76–77), the city has a gallery that stands up to comparison with almost any in Europe.

Collection The National Museum of Ancient Art contains one of Portugal's finest art collections, and ranks second only to the Gulbenkian among Lisbon's galleries and museums. The collection of paintings shows the development of Portuguese art from about the 11th century onwards, and also includes work by several of Europe's greatest artists. There is a wealth of decorative art and silverware, notably Italian ceramics, ecclesiastical vestments, Flemish tapestries, and a monstrance from the Mosteiro (▷ 86–87) in Belém, reputedly

Extraordinary silverwork displayed in the Museu Nacional de Arte Antiga (left); detail of the Adoration of St. Vincent *(middle); ecclesiastical silverware (right); the statue of St. Trinity (below left); part of the stunning art collection at the museum (below middle); the* Temptation of St. Antony *by Hieronymus Bosch (below right)*

made from the first gold brought back from the Indies by Vasco da Gama. Also worth seeing are a decorated chapel, preserved from a convent previously on the site, and the Namban screens, which depict the arrival of the Portuguese in Japan in 1543.

Adoration The museum's most famous painting by far is an altarpiece, the *Painéis de São Vicente de Fora*, or *Adoration of St. Vincent*, thought to be painted by Nuno Gonçalves between 1465 and 1470. The work was discovered only in 1882, dirty and dismembered in a defunct Lisbon church. Its six panels portray around 60 figures paying homage to St. Vincent, Lisbon's patron saint, who is depicted twice. Other treasures include works by Grão Vasco, Frei Carlos, Memling, Holbein, Dürer, Raphael and Velázquez.

THE BASICS

www.ipmuseus.pt
F9
Rua das Janelas Verdes
213 912 800
Wed–Sun 10–1, 2–6, Tue 2–6
Small bar and restaurant
60, 713, 714, 732; tram 15, 18, 25
Santos (Cascais line)
Very good: lift, small steps
Moderate

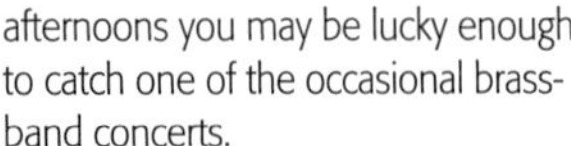

More to See

JARDIM BOTÂNICO

www.jb.ul.pt

Spread across a slope just above Avenida da Liberdade, this oasis is one of the areas of green space you should not miss. Laid out in 1873, it is still the responsibility of the Faculty of Sciences. Mazes of little paved paths wind downhill past masses of exotic plants and trees, all clearly marked. The Rua da Alegria entrance closes early during the week and is closed on weekends.

H6 Rua Escola Politécnica 58-Rua da Alegria 213 921 800 Apr–end Oct Mon–Fri 9–8, Sat–Sun 10–8; Nov–end Mar Mon–Fri 9–6, Sat–Sun 10–6 Rato 758 Inexpensive

JARDIM GUERRA JUNQUEIRO

This easy-going park is better known as the Jardim da Estrela, after the Basílica da Estrela (▷ 59). It is popular with families and has designated areas for kids to play, patches of shade, and a small duck-dotted lake (with a nice adjacent café), which serves as the park's natural focus. There is also a wrought-iron gazebo, and on summer afternoons you may be lucky enough to catch one of the occasional brass-band concerts.

F7 Calçada da Estrela 7am–midnight Café Rato 709, 720, 738; tram 25, 28 Free

MIRADOURO DE SÃO PEDRO DE ALCÂNTARA

Perched on the edge of the Bairro Alto, this belvedere offers sweeping views of the Rossio and Baixa below. Part of the fun here is to travel the old Elevador da Glória, built in 1885.

J7 Rua São Pedro de Alcântara Restauradores 758; Glória elevator

MUSEU DA MARIONETA

www.museudamarioneta.egeac.pt

This fascinating museum displays indigenous puppets from Japan, Thailand, Burma and Indonesia. There are also occasional puppet shows. Housed in the beautifully restored 17th-century Convento das Bernardas.

G8 Rua da Esperança 146 213 942 810 Tue–Sun 10–1, 2–6 60, 713, 727; tram 25 Inexpensive

A peaceful scene at the Jardim Guerra Junqueiro

Gateway to the Jardim Botânico

Across the Tejo

A ferry ride across the Tejo, a short bus ride and a bit of walking gets you out of the city, to a major landmark, the Cristo Rei.

DISTANCE: 4.5km (3 miles) **ALLOW:** 3 hours

CAIS DO SODRÉ
J9 Cais do Sodré

❶ Follow the signs from the metro to the ferry terminal, where you can buy a return ticket to Cacilhas. When you board the ferry try to secure an upstairs window for the best views.

❷ The trip across the river takes 10 minutes, and gives good photo opportunities looking back at the city. You will pass the Ponte 25 de Abril, the huge bridge built in 1966.

❸ On reaching shore turn left in front of the bus station and find stand No. 20. Take bus 101 for Santuário do Cristo Rei, which leaves every 20 minutes.

❹ You can pay the driver on board the bus. The trip to see the massive statue takes about 15 minutes and you will pass through the modern part of bustling Almada.

❺ Once over the brow of the hill you will see the huge statue of Christ.

❻ Inspired by the famous Christ the Redeemer in Rio de Janeiro, Brazil, this monument is awe-inspiring. Leaving the bus stop, walk through the central arch of the buildings in front of the statue.

❼ At its base you will get a feeling of its sheer size, some 110m (360ft) tall. Take the lift inside the statue to the observation platform, reached through the souvenir shop. An amazing vista awaits you across to the city and beyond.

❽ Take the bus back to Almada (3rd or 4th stop) for a wander up to the old town. From here, walk back down the hill to catch the ferry.

END

CAIS DO SODRÉ

Shopping

AMOREIRAS
www.amoreiras.com
Lisbon's first mall is in the Torres das Amoreiras north of the city. This distinctive building was designed by Tomás Taveira, one of Portugal's leading architects. It contains a hotel, 10 cinemas, over 70 cafés and restaurants, and more than 350 shops. Most stay open until late, seven days a week.
F5 Avenida Engenheiro Duarte Pacheco 213 810 200 24, 48, 53, 711, 723

ARQUITECTÓNICA
This is a good place to go if you are looking for avant-garde designer furniture and furnishings.
H6 Rua da Escola Politécnica 94 213 979 605 Rato 758

CASA DAS VELAS DO LORETO
This shop in the Bairro Alto has been producing candles of all shapes and sizes for over 200 years.
J8 Rua do Loreto 53 213 425 387 Baixa-Chiado

DEPOSITO DA MARINHA GRANDE
www.dmg.com.pl
These shops are outlets for Marinha Grande's own reasonably priced glass and china. The firm is long established, and its Atlantis glass is well known in Portugal.
G6 Rua de São Bento 234–242 213 963 234 Rato, Baixa-Chiado 706, 727, 773; tram 25, 28

EL DORADO
Secondhand vintage clothing, mainly from the 1950s, '60s and '70s. It also sells records.
J7 Rua do Norte 23–25 213 423 935 Baixa-Chiado

FÁTIMA LOPES
www.fatima-lopes.com
One of Portugal's most successful designers, whose trademark cutting-edge styles feature sleek body-hugging fabrics.
J7 Rua da Atalaia 36 213 240 546 Baixa-Chiado

BARCELOS COCKS

Although originally from Barcelos in the north, it's hard to avoid the ubiquitous Barcelos Cock painted pottery and wooden models that assault you from every souvenier shop and stall, especially since adopted by the tourist authority as their emblem. The cock's story is a tale told across the Iberian peninsula. A pilgrim heading for Santiago de Compostela was unjustly accused of theft on leaving Barcelos. Despite pleading innocence, he was found guilty and sentenced to death. Looking at the roast cockerel served for the judge's dinner, he invoked the help of St. James, saying that if he were innocent the dead cock would crow. This it promptly did and the man was released.

LIVRARIA BUCHHOLZ
This pleasantly jumbled three-floor shop not only sells a range of English-language books (as well as an excellent range of Portuguese titles), but also is one of the few outlets to sell Portuguese folk and other ethnic music.
H5 Rua Duque de Palmela 4 213 170 580 Marquês de Pombal

MERCADO RIBEIRA
www.espacoribeira.pt
The best food and general market in the city. It's worth visiting just to watch the entertaining standholders. There is a flower market upstairs.
J9 Avenida 24 de Julho Mon–Sat 6am–2pm; flower market 6am–7pm Cais do Sodre

PRÍNCIPE REAL
www.principereal.com
This prestigious firm produces and sells some of the loveliest table linens, cottons and other fabrics in the city. Royalty and all manner of rich and famous clients have patronized the shop. Sheets and tablecloths are good buys, and prices are not as outrageous as you might expect.
H6 Rua da Escola Politécnica 12–14 213 465 945 758

ADEGA DO MACHADO

www.adegamachado.web.pt

Once one of the oldest and most revered of all the *fado* clubs, where now you can experience *fado* and folk dancing in traditional costume, albeit rather touristy.

J7 Rua do Norte 91 213 224 640 Tue–Sun 8pm–3am Baixa-Chiado 758; tram 28

ADEGA DO RIBATEJO

Popular with locals, there are *fado* performances by paid singers and also the cooks or the management take part.

J7 Rua Diário de Notíçias 23 213 468 343 Mon–Sat 8pm–12.30am Baixa-Chiado 758; tram 28

ARCADAS DO FAIA

You are guaranteed to hear good authentic *fado* at this Bairro Alto spot. Also excellent traditional Portuguese cooking.

J7 Rua da Barroca 54–56 213 426 742 Mon–Sat 8pm–2am 758; tram 28

A SEVERA

www.asevera.com

Named after a legendary 19th-century gypsy *fadista*, it attracts many of the big names in the *fado* firmament and charges high prices.

J7 Rua das Gáveas 51–61 213 428 314 Thu–Tue 8pm–3am Baixa-Chiado 758; tram 28

BLUES CAFÉ

A former warehouse on the Doca de Alcântara, in the Alcântara nightlife waterfront district, is now a bar-club-restaurant that serves Cajun food. Live blues two or three nights a week, and DJ dance music at the weekend.

E9 Rua da Cintura do Porta de Lisboa, Armazen H, Navez 213 957 085 Tue–Sat 8.30pm–4am Alcântara Mar (Cascais line from Cais do Sodré) 28, 727; tram 15

WHERE TO GO

For years you had to go no farther than the streets of the Bairro Alto to find a good night out. These days bars and clubs are increasingly farther afield, because of official urban regeneration policies and attempts to take noisy late-night entertainment away from the residential Bairro Alto. Trendy new places have opened on and around the Avenida da 24 de Julho (along the waterfront west of Cais do Sodré), the Alcântara district (notably the fast-growing and increasingly fashionable Doca do Santo Amaro, also on the waterfront, and using refurbished warehouses), and to a lesser extent the fringes of the Alfama and Graça districts east of the heart of the city. Gay bars and clubs cluster around the Rato, on the fringes of the Bairro Alto.

BUDDHA

Near the Doca bars and restaurants, this is a good place to end the evening. Housed in a 1940's maritime terminal with Asian- influenced décor, low tables and Buddhas. Deep house and chilled sounds in the lounge.

Off map at E9 Gare Marítima da Alcântara 30, Docas 213 950 555 Tue–Thu 10pm–4am, Fri–Sat 10pm–6am Alcântara Mar (Cascais line from Cais do Sodré) 28, 727; tram 28E

CAFÉ LUSO

www.cafeluso.pt

Housed in the cellar of a 17th-century palace, Café Luso is one of the most renowned *fado* and folklore restaurants in Lisbon. Many major artists have performed here.

J7 Travessa da Queimada 10 213 422 281 Daily Baixa-Chiado 758; tram 28

FRÁGIL

www.fragil.com.pt

Opened in 1983, this is one of the oldest, most popular and trendy of the Bairro's many club-bars.

J7 Rua da Atalaia 126 213 469 578 Tue–Sat 11pm–4am (Oct–May Thu–Sat only) 758; tram 28

HOT CLUBE JAZZ

www.hcp.pt

Long thought of as Lisbon's best place for jazz. It hosts Portuguese and visiting performers.

J6 Praça de Alegria 39, off Avenida da Liberdade 213 467 369 Check website for concerts and sessions; sessions usually start at 11pm Avenida

KREMLIN

www.grupo-k.pt

Hip and difficult to get into, so dress to impress. Gets going after 2am and closes about 7am.

G9 Rua Escadinhas da Praia 5 213 525 867 Wed–Sat midnight–dawn Santos (Cascais line from Cais do Sodré) 28, 727; tram 15, 18

O SENHOR VINHO

www.srvinho.com

In Lapa, this celebrated club is west of the tourist haunts of the Alfama and Bairro Alto. As a result it is more authentic—though not necessarily much cheaper—than other clubs.

F8 Rua do Meio à Lapa 18 213 972 681 Mon–Sat 7.30pm–2am 773; tram 25, 28

PAVILHÃO CHINÊS

Covered with a jumble of fans, china, sheet music and other miscellaneous *objets d'art*, this place sells reasonably priced drinks and cocktails.

H7 Rua Dom Pedro V 89 213 424 729 Mon–Sat 6pm–2am; Sun 9pm–2am Restauradores 758

PLATEAU

If you have no joy at Kremlin (▷ this page), or want something a little less trendy and with more mainstream rock and pop, this is the place.

G9 Rua Escadinhas da Praia 7 213 965 116 Wed–Sat Santos (Cascais line) from Cais do Sodré 28, 727; tram 15, 18

SNOB

A quieter, classier Bairro Alto bar with wooden booths, leather seats and soothing green baize.

H7 Rua do Século 178 213 463 723 Daily 4.30pm–3am 758; tram 28

SOLAR DO VINHO DO PORTO

www.ivp.pt

Feeling more like a private club than a bar, the port wine institute offers respite from the bustle of the Bairro Alto. Choose from an extensive list of port wines which can be tasted by the glass in the comfort of an armchair.

J7 Rua de São Pedro de Alcântara 45 213 475 707 Mon–Sat 11am–midnight Baixa-Chiado, Restauradores

COVER CHARGE

***Fado* houses don't charge admission, but nearly all make a cover charge. This usually buys you a couple of drinks. Performances usually start around 9pm, the real action may begin only between 11pm and midnight. In theory, in most top Lisbon clubs there is no official charge at the door but drinks carry a surcharge once inside. In practice, women are rarely asked to pay at the door while the fate of their male companions depends on the mood of the doorman.**

SPEAKEASY

www.speakeasy-bar.com

Good-quality live jazz, with the occasional big name, two or three times weekly at this bar-restaurant at the Doca de Alcântara.

E9 Armazém 115, Cais das Oficinas, Rocha Conde de Óbidos 213 964 257 Sun–Thu 8pm–3am, Fri–Sat 8pm–4am Alcântara Mar (Cascais line) from Cais do Sodré 28, 727; tram 15

TIMPANAS

www.timpanas.pt

The show in this *fado* house in the Alcântara district is organized with dinner and folk dancing rather than spontaneous *fado*, but there's still some good singing.

Off map Rua Gilberto Rola 22–24 213 906 655 Closed Wed Alcântara Mar (Cascais line from Cais do Sodré) 28, 727; tram 15, 18

TRUMPS

www.trumps.pt

Lisbon's most popular gay club, with two separate dance areas playing different sorts of music.

G6 Rua da Imprensa Nacional 104b 213 971 059 Fri–Sat 11.45pm–6am (hours can be erratic) Rato 758

Restaurants

PRICES

Prices are approximate, based on a 3-course meal for one person.

€€€ over €25
€€ €15–€25
€ under €15

ALFAIA (€)

A busy and popular restaurant, especially for lunch. You need search no farther for a reasonably priced meal in a typical Bairro Alto establishment.
J7 Travessa da Queimada 22 213 461 232 Mon–Sat lunch, dinner; Sun dinner only Restauradores

ALI-À-PAPA (€€)

If you fancy an alternattive to solid Portuguese cooking, try this Moroccan restaurant. The evocative draperies and candles provide an authentic setting for the aromatic cuisine that focuses on quality ingredients.
J7 Rua da Atalaia 95 213 474 143 Wed–Mon dinner only 758; tram 28

BOTA ALTA (€€)

Attractive and rustic eaterie in the Bairro Alto. Big portions of traditional cooking draw the crowds.
J7 Travessa da Queimada 35–37 213 427 959 Mon–Fri lunch, dinner; Sat lunch only Restauradores–Elevador da Glória or Baixa-Chiado 758; tram 28

CASA DA COMIDA (€€€)

www.casadacomida.pt
Thought of as being among Lisbon's finest French-Portuguese restaurants, this is a good place to treat yourself, though it is well northwest of the city centre. The setting is wonderful—a former mansion in a little square—and the fresh ingredients delectable. In summer you can eat outside.
G6 Travessa das Amoireiras 1, off Rua Alexandre Herculano 213 885 376 Tue–Fri lunch, dinner; Sat–Mon dinner only Rato 6, 9, 74

COLONIAL INFLUENCE

Colonial days may be long gone but their inheritance lives on, especially in Portugal's cuisine. As the Portuguese returned from the ex-colonies they brought with them such dishes as *moamba* from Angola, *cachupa* from Caboverde, and the tiger prawns grilled in *piri-piri* sauce from Mozambique. From Goa came the *chamuças* and curries and from Brazil the roast meats of the *picanha* and the famous bean feast known as *feijoada brasileira*. All these and many more can now be found around the city, both in their own typical restaurants and dotted through the menus of traditionally Portuguese establishments, often opened by those who spent years abroad.

CASA FAZ FRIO (€€)

On the northern edge of the Bairro Alto, this is one of Lisbon's lovelier and more traditional restaurants. Known for its low prices and excellent seafood.
H7 Rua Dom Pedro V 96 213 461 860 Mon–Sat lunch, dinner Restauradores–Elevador da Glória 758

CLUBE DOS JORNALISTAS (€€–€€€)

This pretty restaurant with its flower-filled patio is housed in the Portuguese journalists' club. Innovative Catalan cooking draws a crowd, and the home-made ice cream is very popular. Reservations are recommended.
F8 Ruas das Trinas 129 r/c, Lapa 213 977 138 Mon–Sat lunch, dinner 713, 773; tram 25

COMIDA DE SANTO (€€–€€€)

www.comidadesanto.com.pt
This lively Brazilian restaurant is known for its powerful cocktails and South American-influenced Portuguese dishes. Try the delicious *feijoada* (bean stew).
H6 Calçada Engenheiro Miguel Pais 39, off Rua da Escola Politécnica 213 963 339 Daily lunch, dinner Rato 758

CONFRARIA AT YORK HOUSE (€€€)
www.yorkhouselisboa.com
Tucked away in a 17th-century former Carmelite convent, this restaurant, with its oasis-like courtyard, has transformed its cuisine over the last few years. An extensive selection of traditional predominently Portuguese dishes are served with refined elegance.
F9 Rua das Janelas Verdes 32 213 962 435 Daily lunch, dinner 60, 727; tram 25

CONVENTUAL (€€€)
This restaurant is finely decorated with antique and modern religious art and the famous Arraiolos carpets. Its religious theme continues in the names of its dishes, such as Pope of Avignon snails, and in its excellent *doces conventuais*, sweet, eggy desserts which were originally made by nuns.
G7 Praça das Flores 45 213 909 246 Tue–Fri lunch, dinner; Sat–Mon dinner only. Closed Aug Rato 773

CULTURA DO CHÁ (€)
For a break whilst you are exploring the maze of the Bairro Alto, drop into this cosy tea shop for a selection of fine teas or coffee and a selection of homemade cakes and savoury snacks.
J8 Rua das Salgadeiras 38 213 430 272 12–9.30 Baixa-Chiado

ENOTECA CHAFARIZ DO VINHO (€€)
www.chafarizdovinho.com
In the beautiful 18th-century building known as the Chafariz do Vinho, this is an excellent place for a tapas-style plate of ham, spicy sausage and cheeses, all washed down with a glass of wine.
H6 Rua da Mâe d'Água 213 422 079 Tue–Sun dinner from 6pm Restauradores– Elevador da Glória 758

ESPAÇO LISBOA (€€–€€€)
It is worth eating here just for the architecture. In an old factory building, this huge restaurant is decorated with thousands of beautiful tiles. The menu focuses on Portuguese cooking.
Off map Rua da Cozinha Económica 16 213 610 212 Daily lunch, dinner Alcântara (Cascais line) from Cais do Sodré 738; tram 15, 18

BASICS

Hors d'oeuvres are *acepipes*. Breakfast is *pequeno almoço*, lunch *almoço* and dinner *jantar*. Soups are typically inexpensive and filling as a first course. Meat (*carne*) and poultry (*aves*) are usually simply grilled or fried: roast or barbecued chicken is a particularly tasty Portuguese dish. Fish (*peixe*) and seafood (*mariscos*), though, are preeminent in Lisbon. Salt cod (*bacalhau*) and sardines (*sardinhas*) are virtually the national dishes. Vegetables are *legumes* and salad *salada*. Bread is *pão*.

FIDALGO (€€)
www.restaurantefidalgo.com
This popular rendezvous for media types is trendier than most of the Bairro Alto restaurants. The menu offers great fish dishes.
J7 Rua da Barroca 27 213 422 900 Mon–Sat lunch, dinner Baixa-Chiado 758; tram 28

O CHÁ DA LAPA (€)
Relax on red velvet sofas while indulging in delicious freshly made cakes and biscuits at this traditional tea shop. Tasty quiches for lunch.
F9 Rua do Olival 8–10 213 900 888 Daily 9–7 60, 727; tram 25

OLIVIER (€€)
www.restaurante-olivier.com
A good choice if you want to try authentic national cooking. It's renowned for its Portuguese dishes such as *bacalhau* (salt cod) and *arroz de pato* (rice with duck).
J8 Rua do Alecrim 23 213 422 916 Mon–Sat dinner only Baixa-Chiado 758

PAP'AÇORDA (€€€)
Trendy, predominantly young, gay, arty clientele frequents this restaurant in a converted bakery. Try the *açorda* (bread soup). J7 Rua da Atalaia 57–9 213 464 811 Tue–Sat lunch, dinner; closed first 2 weeks Jul and Nov Baixa-Chiado 758; tram 28

PICANHA (€€)
Excellent Brazilian grilled meats, *farofa* (manioc), *feijão* (beans) and other Brazilian delights. Try the *caipirinhas*, alcoholic lemon punches. F9 Rua das Janelas Verdes 96 213 975 401 Mon–Fri lunch, dinner; Sat, Sun dinner only 60, 727; tram 25

PORTUGÁLIA (€€)
One of the several Portugália *cervejarias* around the city—this one enjoys the best location. A limited selection of good, fast food; open until late. H9 Doca de Santos, Cintura do Porto de Lisboa, Armazem 63 213 422 138 Daily lunch, dinner Cais do Sodré 36, 40, 44, 794

PRIMAVERA (€)
This tiny spotless restaurant (reservations are recommended) is a bastion of honest Portuguese cooking. Friendly waiters do their best to ensure you enjoy your meal. J8 Travessa da Espera 34 213 420 477 Tue–Sat lunch, dinner, Mon dinner only Baixa-Chiado 758, 790; tram 28

RESTAURANTE 33 (€€–€€€)
Close to many of the Avenida hotels and decorated in the style of an English hunting lodge, this restaurant includes such dishes as smoked salmon, lobster or pepper steak. Live piano music is often played while you eat. H5 Rua Alexandre Herculano 33A 213 546 079 Mon–Fri lunch, dinner; Sat dinner only Marquês de Pombal 709

PORT

Port is a Douro region wine that is sweet because brandy has been added at a certain point to stop the grape sugar turning into alcohol. It may be red or white. Young red port, or *tinto*, is the most common, and is distinctive and very fruity. Reds are used to make blended ports, the blend comprising ports from different years, the quality depending on the wines used. Reds are also the basis of vintage, ruby and tawny ports (▷ 33). White port, or *branco*, is sometimes fermented again to remove the sweetness. If chilled, this dry white port makes a delicious apéritif.

RIBADOURO (€–€€)
www.cervejariaribadouro.pt
Eat informally at the bar or downstairs in the main restaurant. Great seafood. H6 Corner of Rua do Salitre and Avenida da Liberdade 155 213 549 411 Daily lunch, dinner Avenida All services to Avenida da Liberdade

SOLAR DOS NUNES (€€)
This small restaurant serves game, including wild boar, partridge and hare in season. Also try the excellent-value steaks. Off map Rua dos Lusíadas 70 213 647 359 Mon–Sat lunch, dinner; closed 2 weeks Aug 738; tram 15, 18

ÚLTIMO TANGO (€–€€)
In the Bairro Alto, this Argentinian restaurant serves excellent steaks and a fine selection of Argentinian wines. J7 Rua Diário de Notícias 62 213 420 341 Mon–Sat dinner only 758, 790; tram 28

XL (€€€)
The ocre-painted walls, rustic furniture and antique curiosities give this popular restaurant a homely feel. Camembert, in breadcrumbs with raspberry sauce, and soufflés are their forte. F7 Calçada da Estrela 57 213 956 118 Daily dinner only 6, 13, 706, 727, 773; tram 25, 28

Northwest of Avenida da Liberdade, stretching to the huge expanse of the Monsanto Forest park, the district of São Sebastião encompasses some of the city's major attractions and green spaces.

Sights **76–82**

Top 25 **TOP 25**

Museu Calouste Gulbenkian ▷ **76**

Palácio dos Marqueses de Fronteira ▷ **78**

Centro de Arte Moderna ▷ **80**

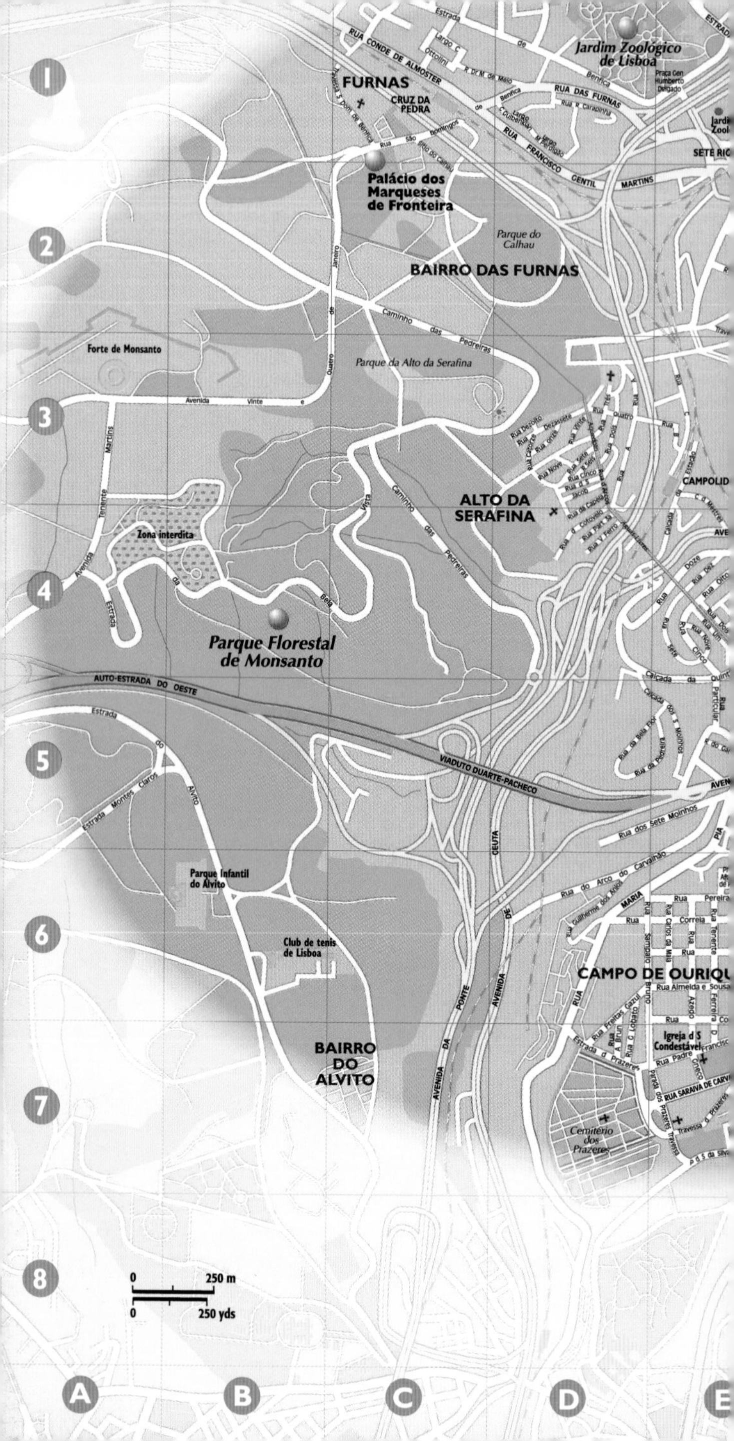

Jardim Zoológico de Lisboa
FURNAS
CRUZ DA PEDRA
RUA CONDE DE ALMOSTER
RUA DAS FURNAS
RUA FRANCISCO GENTIL MARTINS
SETE RIOS
Palácio dos Marqueses de Fronteira
Parque do Calhau
BAIRRO DAS FURNAS
Caminho das Pedreiras
Forte de Monsanto
Parque da Alto da Serafina
Avenida Vinte e Quatro de Janeiro
ALTO DA SERAFINA
CAMPOLIDE
Zona interdita
Estrada da Bela Vista
Parque Florestal de Monsanto
AUTO-ESTRADA DO OESTE
VIADUTO DUARTE-PACHECO
Estrada do Alvito
Estrada Montes Claros
Rua dos Sete Moinhos
Rua do Arco do Carvalhão
Parque Infantil do Alvito
Club de tenis de Lisboa
CAMPO DE OURIQUE
AVENIDA DA PONTE
AVENIDA DE CEUTA
Igreja d S Condestável
RUA SARAIVA DE CARVALHO
BAIRRO DO ALVITO
Cemitério dos Prazeres
Estrada d Prazeres
1
2
3
4
5
6
7
8
0
250 m
0
250 yds
A
B
C
D
E

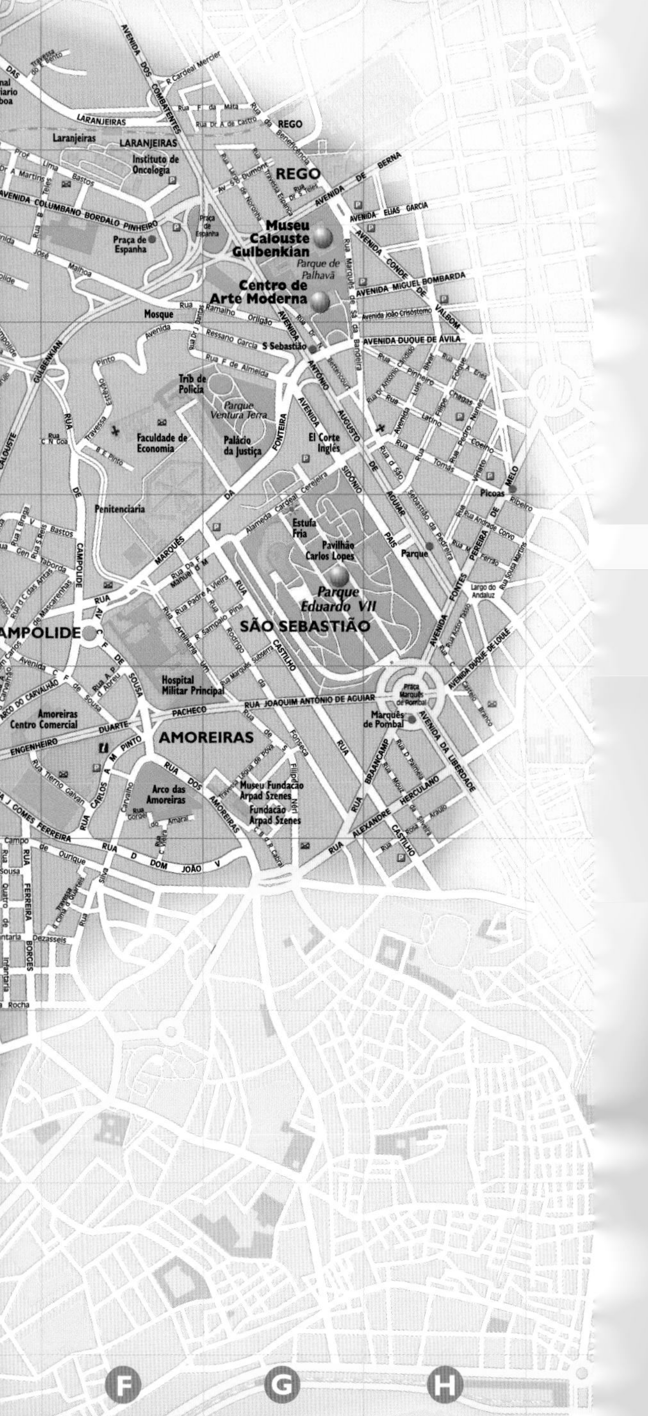

Museu Calouste Gulbenkian

HIGHLIGHTS

- Rembrandt paintings
- Islamic ceramics
- Lalique jewellery and glass
- Carpets
- French ivory diptychs

TIPS

- Leave time to enjoy the gardens.
- Make use of the touch-screen computers.

If given the job of putting together an art gallery with unlimited funds, you would come up with something close to the Gulbenkian. Its range is complete, from ancient to modern, famous to obscure and from east to west.

Bequest to the nation The Gulbenkian is Portugal's greatest museum. Run by the Fundação Calouste Gulbenkian, it is one of the countless artistic and cultural initiatives financed by a bequest from Calouste Gulbenkian (1869–1955), an Armenian oil magnate. It was built between 1964 and 1969 by architects Alberto Passoal, Pedro Cid and Ruy Athouguia. Gulbenkian's extensive private art collection makes up the bulk of the museum's collection, which is divided into two sections: the first deals

Portrait of Helena Fourment (c1630–32) by Rubens (left); stunning display of 14th-century mosque lamps (middle); superb peacock inlaid with opals and diamonds by René Lalique (right); exterior of the museum (below left); head of Alexander the Great (below middle); picture gallery (below right)

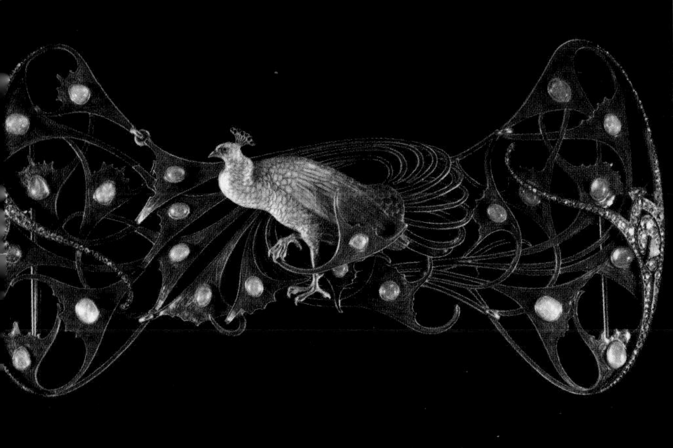

with ancient and Oriental exhibits, the second with European art and objects.

Stunning collection The European section embraces paintings, sculptures and the decorative arts. Exhibits are arranged chronologically and, wherever possible, according to school and nationality. The paintings include works by Manet, Degas, Renoir, Van Dyck, Frans Hals, Turner and Gainsborough. Pride of place goes to Rembrandt's *Alexander the Great* and captivating *Portrait of an Old Man*. Among the wealth of tapestries, furniture, silverware and other beautiful objects, look out in particular for the stunning jewellery by René Lalique (in a reverentially darkened room at the end of the gallery). In the ancient and Oriental sections the highlights include Chinese porcelain, Japanese lacquer work and silk and wool carpets.

THE BASICS

www.museu.gulbenkian.pt
G2
Avenida de Berna 45A
217 823 000
Tue–Sun 10–5.45. Closed public hols
Café
São Sebastião/Praça de Espanha
16, 56,718, 726, 742
Excellent
Moderate; free on Sun
Downhill from São Sebastião metro, turn right after 300m (330 yards)

Palácio dos Marqueses de Fronteira

HIGHLIGHTS

- Battle Room
- Delft, or Dining, Room
- Gallery of Arts (tiled terrace)
- Chapel
- Gardens
- Doze de Inglaterra
- Statues of the Nine Muses
- Statues of Portugal's first 15 kings

TIP

- The gardens are not included in a tour when it is raining.

Even if you are usually a little lazy when it comes to trekking out to the suburbs of a city, the beautiful Italianate gardens and captivating tiles make the journey to the Fronteira Palace more than worthwhile.

Isolated beauty A metro ride from the Rossio drops you close to the Fronteira Palace in an area of somewhat moribund modern housing and half-finished roads. The palace and its gardens, an oasis of beauty in this wasteland, were founded in 1670 as a hunting lodge by João Mascarenhas, the first Marquês de Fronteira. The palace is still privately owned, but guided tours take you around some half-dozen rooms, notably the Battle Room, whose tiled decoration depicts scenes from the War of Restoration. This campaign brought to an end 60 years of Spanish domination in Portugal between

The formal gardens, laid out in the 17th century (left); detail of azulejos *(tiles) and niched statues on the exterior of the palace (right); intricate detail of the Doze de Inglaterra (below left); part of the panels of the gallant horsemen of the Doze de Inglaterra (below right)*

1581 and 1640. Fronteira was a general, and played a prominent part in the war.

Gardens The palace's Italianate gardens, full of fountains, topiary terraces, little lakes and a dense green web of clipped hedging, are a delight, not least because of the *azulejos*, or tiles, which decorate virtually every suitable surface. You will already have seen a wide variety of tiles in the palace, including some of the first Delft tiles imported into Portugal (in the 17th century). In the gardens, there are benches, walls and ornamental pools swathed with tiles depicting all manner of subjects. The most eye-catching are the life-size depictions of the Doze de Inglaterra, 12 gallant horsemen who, according to the legend, sailed to England to fight for the glory of rescuing 12 damsels in distress.

THE BASICS

C2
Largo de São Domingos de Benfica 1
217 782 023
Palace and gardens: guided tours Jun–end Sep Mon–Sat 10.30, 11, 11.30 and 12; Oct–end May Mon–Sat 11 and 12. Gardens only: Mon–Sat 11–1, 2.15–5
Sete Rios
70
Poor
Gardens: moderate. Palace and gardens: expensive
The palace can only be visited on an official tour

Centro de Arte Moderna

The Centro de Arte Moderna and its outdoor sculpture exhibits are set in parkland

THE BASICS

www.camjap.gulbenkian.pt
G2
Rua Dr Nicolau de Bettencourt
217 823 474
Tue–Sun 10–6 (last entry 5.45)
São Sebastião/Praça de Espanha
16, 56, 718, 726, 742
Good
Moderate or joint ticket with Gulbenkian Museum (expensive). Free on Sun

HIGHLIGHTS

- Henry Moore
- Amadeu de Souza-Cardoso
- Guilherme Santa Rita
- Paula Rego
- Vieira da Silva
- Julio Pomar
- Costa Pinheiro

Names of modern Portuguese artists will be unfamiliar to most people, but there's no better place to become acquainted with their work than this state-of-the-art gallery sponsored by the Calouste Gulbenkian Foundation.

Parkland gem Lisbon's Centre for Modern Art lies just around the corner from the better-known Museu Calouste Gulbenkian (▷ 76–77). Like its near neighbour, it was made possible by the legacy of Calouste Gulbenkian, the Armenian oil magnate, who left his art collection and a slice of his fortune to Portugal. The building is set in the same park and is in a beautiful modern structure designed by the British architect Sir Leslie Martin. It opened in 1983. The museum's airy exhibition space—all clean lines and abundant greenery—is a pleasure in itself, admirably complementing a collection of over 10,000 works of art.

National collection The parkland surrounding the museum is scattered with sculptures, of which the most notable is the *Reclining Woman* by Henry Moore, near the main entrance. Inside, the gallery's eminent Portuguese painters include Amadeu de Souza-Cardoso and Guilherme Santa Rita, both of whom were influenced by the Italian Futurists. In acknowledging the work of foreign painters, the pair were typical of Portuguese artists, most of whom worked or studied abroad. By following such foreign styles and not establishing their own movement few artists from Portugal are said to have strongly influenced the evolution of modern art.

More to See

JARDIM ZOOLÓGICO DE LISBOA

www.zoo.pt

Lisbon's zoo has been much improved over recent years and is in appealing surroundings in the former Parque das Laranjeiras, an old estate whose rose gardens, ponds and formal flower beds have been carefully preserved among the animals. The upper, northern part of the park is wilder and less cultivated, with places for picnics and leisurely exploration. In particular the Miradouro dos Moinhos (the Mill Belvedere) and the cable car both provide a broad panorama across parkland and the rest of the city. The park also has an eccentric little cemetery for dogs.

D1 Praça Marechal Humberto Delgado, Sete Rios 217 232 900 Apr–end Sep daily 10–8; Oct–end Mar daily 10–6 Café Jardim Zoológico 16, 54, 746, 758, 768 Expensive

PARQUE EDUARDO VII

At the northern end of Avenida da Liberdade, the park revolves around two broad, mosaic-paved boulevards, which in turn are intersected by tiny walkways and carefully manicured little hedgerows. There are panoramic views from Rua Alameda Cardeal Cerejeira on the northern side, and the wonderful cool and hot houses are lovely places to spend a tranquil half hour away from the city hustle and bustle.

G4 Praça Marquês de Pombal Café Parque, Marquês de Pombal 2, 12, 22, 720 and many other services to Praça Marquês de Pombal

PARQUE FLORESTAL DE MONSANTO

This enormous area of parkland on the western fringes of Lisbon is probably the city's most positive legacy of Salazar (▷ 125) but it is not recommended for walking. It is poorly kept and overgrown and some parts are dangerous and insalubrious by day or night. However, it is worth visiting for the fine views from the Miradouro de Monsanto and Miradouro dos Montes Claros.

A1–C8 West of Avenida de Ceuta

Perfect tranquillity in the Jardim Zoológico de Lisboa

Belém

A western suburb beside the Tejo and once a prime anchorage spot from where overseas expeditions set sail. Today, fascinating museums and monuments and spacious promenades and gardens define the area.

Sights	**86–95**
Restaurants	**96**

Top 25 TOP 25

Mosteiro dos Jerónimos ▷ **86**

Museu de Marinha ▷ **88**

Museu Nacional dos Coches ▷ **90**

Padrão dos Descobrimentos ▷ **91**

Torre de Belém ▷ **92**

RESTÉLO
BELÉM
Avenida das Descobertas
Avenida do Restelo
Avenida da Torre de Belém
Avenida da Índia
Avenida de Brasilia
Rua Gonçalo Velho Cabral
Rua Gonçalo Nunes
Rua Diogo de Teive
Rua Gonçalo Sintre
Rua Rodrigo Rebelo
Rua A Esteves
Rua António de Saldanha
Rua Pero de Alenquer
Rua Pero da Covilhã
Rua de Alcolena
Rua Gil Eanes
Museu Nac de Etnologia
Ermida San Jerónimo
Jardim Ducla Sorres
Praça de Goa
Praça d Damão
Praça de Diu
Praça de Malaca
Rua Pacheco Pereira
Rua Dom Francisco de Almeida
Rua Dom Lourenço de Almeida
Rua Duarte
Rua São Francisco de Xavier
Rua Tristão da Cunha
Rua Dom Cristóvão da Gama
R Ant d Abreu
Rua de Pedrouços
Rua da Praia de Pedrouços
Rua Fernão Mendes Pinto
Vila Correia
Rua J Bastos
Rua Bartolomeu Dias
Rua da Praia do Bom Sucesso
Planetário Calouste Gulbenkian
Museu de Marinha
Centro Cultural de Belém
Doca do Bom Sucesso
Forte do Bom Sucesso
Torre de Belém
0
250 m
0
250 yds
1
2
3
4
a
b

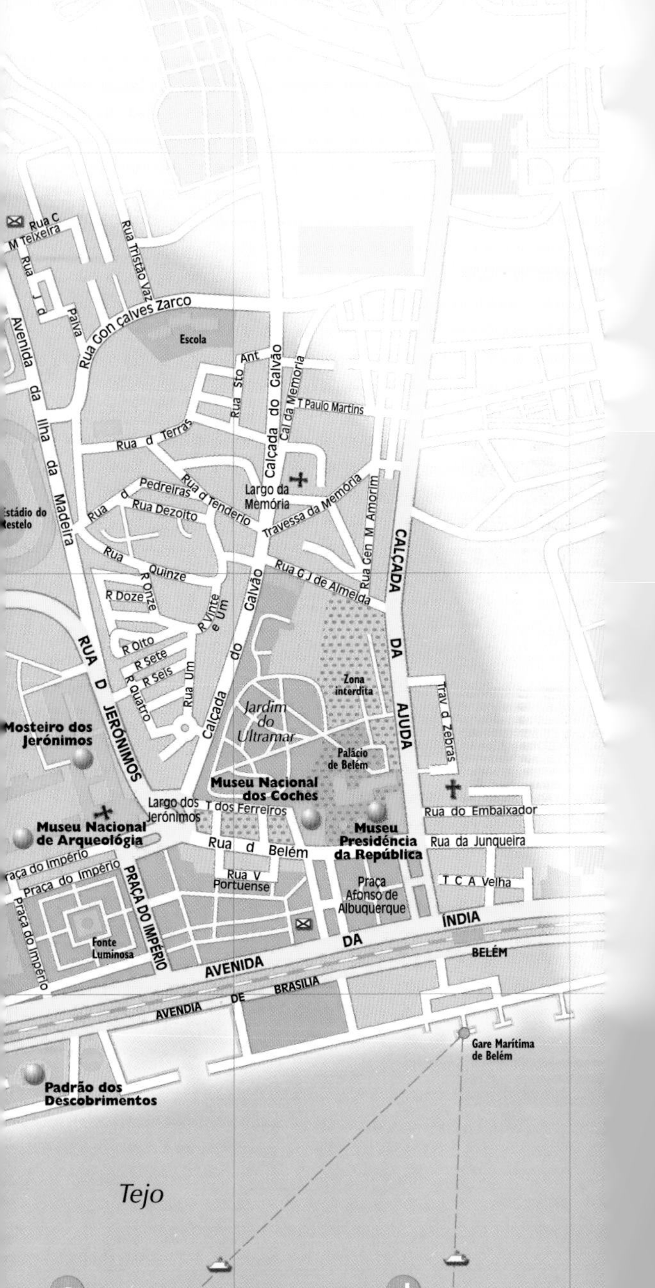

Rua C M Teixeira
Rua Tristão Vaz
Rua J d Paiva
Rua Gon çalves Zarco
Escola
Avenida da Ilha da Madeira
Rua Sto Ant
Calçada do Galvão
Cal da Memória
T Paulo Martins
Rua d Terras
Largo da Memória
Rua d Pedreiras
Rua d Tenderio
Rua Dezoito
Travessa da Memória
Rua Gen M Amorim
Estádio do Restelo
Rua Quinze
Rua G J de Almeida
CALÇADA DA AJUDA
R Doze
R Onze
R Vinte e Um
RUA D JERÓNIMOS
R Oito
R Sete
R Seis
R Quatro
Rua Um
Calçada do Galvão
Zona interdita
Jardim do Ultramar
Trav d Zebras
Mosteiro dos Jerónimos
Palácio de Belém
Museu Nacional dos Coches
Largo dos Jerónimos
T dos Ferreiros
Rua do Embaixador
Museu Nacional de Arqueología
Museu Presidência da República
Rua d Belém
Rua da Junqueira
Praça do Império
Rua V Portuense
Praça Afonso de Albuquerque
T C A Velha
PRAÇA DO IMPÉRIO
ÍNDIA
DA
Fonte Luminosa
BELÉM
AVENIDA
AVENDIA DE BRASILIA
Gare Marítima de Belém
Padrão dos Descobrimentos
Tejo
c
d

Mosteiro dos Jerónimos

HIGHLIGHTS

- South door
- West door
- Fan vaulting
- Nave
- Monument to Vasco da Gama
- Transept star vaulting
- Choir stalls

TIP

- The monastery is always besieged by tour buses. Arrive early, visit during lunch time or wait until late afternoon to escape the buses.

There are no greater buildings in Lisbon than those of the Mosteiro dos Jerónimos, a glorious monastic complex whose carved stonework and magnificent cloisters rival the finest Gothic and Renaissance work.

Praising the explorers The present monastery is built over the site of a small chapel built by Henry the Navigator in 1460 to provide spiritual solace to the many seafarers who embarked on voyages of discovery from Belém. The new church was begun by Manuel I in 1502 to celebrate Vasco da Gama's successful voyage to the Indies, da Gama having held a vigil in Henry's chapel prior to his 1497 expedition. Some 50 years were to elapse before the building was completed, and during this time several architects worked on the project, hence the Gothic, Manueline and

The tomb of poet Luís de Camões basks in the sun inside the monastery (left); detail of a stained-glass window in the monastery church of Santa Maria (middle); the bell tower of the monastery (below middle); intricate detail of the ornate façade of Jerónimos monastery, displaying the Manueline style of architecture (right)

Renaissance mixture of the church's artistic and architectural styles.

Treasures The monastery's treasures begin with the magnificent south door, whose wealth of decoration focuses on the figure of Henry the Navigator, and the contrasting west door, where the protagonists are Manuel I, his wife, Dona Maria, and the pair's respective patron saints. Inside are soaring aisles and a vast, breathtaking array of carved stone, reaching a climax in the sweep of fan vaulting over the nave. Search out da Gama's tomb, beneath a gallery near the church's entrance, and then make for the adjoining cloisters, one of Portugal's great architectural set pieces. The two-level ensemble, and the lower tier in particular, is a feast of outstanding carving, the pillars and vaults embellished with a wealth of intricately sculpted stone.

THE BASICS

www.mosteirojeronimos.pt
c3
Praça do Império
213 620 034
May–end Sep Tue–Sun 10–6; Oct–end Apr Tue–Sun 10–5 (last entry 30 minutes earlier)
28, 714, 727, 729, 751; tram 15
Belém (Cascais line) from Cais do Sodré
Poor
Church: free. Cloisters: moderate, free Sun until 2pm
Tram 15 stops outside the monastery. The return stop is 150m (163 yards) east, opposite Casa dos Pastéis

Museu de Marinha

TOP 25

HIGHLIGHTS

- State barges (Pavilhão das Galeotas)
- Model boats
- Statue of Archangel Raphael
- Cabins of the *Amélia*
- Maps

TIPS

- Plan your visit using the guide. With so much to see the museum can be daunting.
- Don't expect state-of-the-art exhibits; this is an old-fashioned setup.

Lisbon's excellent maritime museum is irresistible, even if you don't admire boats. It is one of the most important of its kind in Europe, and fully captures the glory of Portugal's long and distinguished history of seafaring.

Seafaring nation It seems only right that Lisbon's maritime museum should be in Belém, for it was from the sheltered port nearby that many of the great Portuguese explorers embarked on their voyages of discovery. Today the museum occupies both the west wing of the Mosteiro dos Jerónimos (▷ 86–87) and part of the nearby Galeotas Pavilion—a modern building that is home to the Planetário Calouste Gulbenkian (▷ 94). The former contains a collection of model boats and other maritime ephemera, the latter houses the

The main entrance to Lisbon's Maritime Museum (far left); arched gallery housing displays of model ships (left); remains from the wreck of the Nossa Senhora dos Martires, *1606 (right); one of the stunning royal barges (below left); the Queen's Cabin on board the royal yacht* Amélia *(below right)*

larger exhibits, such as a full-size craft, planes and several impressive royal barges.

Maritime history The bulk of the museum's more venerable exhibits were provided by a private bequest in 1948. So many items were lost or destroyed in the 1755 earthquake that it was not easy to find early objects for the museum. Much of the collection proceeds thematically, from the era of the Age of Great Discoveries onwards. The oldest exhibit is a wooden figure representing the Archangel Raphael, which accompanied Vasco da Gama on his pioneering voyage to the Indies in 1497. From the 19th century comes the ornate splendour of royal yachts, including a reconstruction of a sumptuous cabin from the *Amélia*, built for Carlos I. There is also a section devoted to the Orient and other maritime memorabilia.

THE BASICS

www.museumarinha.pt

c3

Praça do Império

213 620 019

Apr–end Sep Tue–Sun 10–6; Oct–end Mar Tue–Sun 10–5. Closed public hols

28, 714, 727, 729, 751; tram 15

Belém (Cascais line) from Cais do Sodré

Very good

Moderate, free Sun until 1pm

Entrance at western end of Mosteiro dos Jerónimos

Museu Nacional dos Coches

A sumptuous carriage (right) at the Coach Museum (left)

THE BASICS

www.museudoscoches-ipmuseus.pt
d3
Praça Afonso de Albuquerque
213 610 850
Tue–Sun 10–6 (last entry 5.30). Closed public hols
28, 714, 727, 729, 751; tram 15
Belém (Cascais line) from Cais do Sodré
Poor
Moderate, free Sun until 2pm

HIGHLIGHTS

- Painted ceiling vaults
- Coaches of the Marquês de Frontes
- Dom João V's state coach
- Dom José I's state coach
- King Carlos I's miniature carriage
- Maria Anna's royal carriage

It is difficult to imagine that a coach museum could be one of Lisbon's most visited sights until you see for yourself the sheer glory of its beautifully embellished coaches and carriages.

Travel in style Lisbon's National Coach Museum is one of the best collections of its type in the world. For the Portuguese royalty and aristocracy, coaches and carriages were never merely modes of transport, but were used to proclaim the wealth and taste of their owners. As a result, many were painted, gilded and decorated to a magnificent degree, particularly those used for state or ceremonial occasions. The museum, founded by Queen Amélia in 1904, is in the former riding academy and stables of the Palácio do Belém, a royal palace begun around 1726 by Dom João V. Today the palace proper, which is not open to visitors, is the official residence of the Portuguese president.

Rich collection Three of the museum's most splendid coaches are those built in 1716 for the Marquês de Frontes, Portugal's ambassador to Pope Clement XI and the Holy See. Constructed in Italy, the coaches are decorated with allegorical scenes representing Portuguese military and maritime triumphs. Other highlights include many cabs, prams and sedans; the royal carriage of Dom José I; a miniature carriage built for King Carlos I as a child; and Maria Anna of Austria's coach, built for her by her brother when she married King João V. If the museum has a fault it is that there are just too many coaches.

Looking out to sea—the impressive Monument to the Discoveries has intricate carvings

Padrão dos Descobrimentos

It must have taken courage to impose a vast modern monument on an area as historical as Belém, but this huge white waterfront edifice provides a dramatic and dignified landmark.

Maritime pride The Monument to the Discoveries was erected in 1960 during the Salazar dictatorship. It marked the 500th anniversary of the death of Henry the Navigator, the prince who laid the foundation of Portugal's wide-reaching empire through his energetic backing of projects such as a maritime school in the Algarve. The monument has been criticized for its vaguely fascist design and obviously nationalist intent, but it is nonetheless an architectural triumph, imposing itself on the Belém waterfront. Its jutting triangular pediment represents the prow of a ship, while the trio of curving forms above symbolizes billowing sails. Rising over these is a redoubtable blockhouse tower, reaching some 52m (170ft) above the quayside.

Figures The monument's rigid lines are softened by a group of sculpted figures crowded on the pediment's sloping prow. Behind Henry, who holds a ship in his hands, stands Manuel I, the king who reigned from 1495 to 1521, during the height of Portugal's voyages of discovery. He is shown holding an armillary sphere, one of his regal symbols. Other characters include Luís de Camões, one of Portugal's most famous poets, who is depicted holding verses. A lift runs to the top of the monument.

THE BASICS

www.padraodescobrimentos.egeac.pt

c4

Avenida de Brasília

213 031 950

May–end Sep 10–6.30; Oct–end Apr 10–5.30. Closed public hols

28, 714, 727, 729, 751; tram 15

Belém (Cascais line) from Cais do Sodré

Good

Moderate, free Sun until 2pm

HIGHLIGHTS

- Henry the Navigator
- Views from balcony
- Mosaic map

Torre de Belém

TOP 25

DID YOU KNOW?

- The Torre de Belém was declared a World Heritage Site by the United Nations in 1983.

TIPS

- The stairs up the Torre are steep and narrow and you may have to wait for access.
- To avoid the coach parties, arrive when it first opens.

Few buildings are as charming or evocative as the Torre de Belém, a capricious architectural confection of towers, turrets and battlements, whose ramparts are washed by the River Tejo on three sides.

National landmark Lisbon's Belém tower is not only a masterpiece of Renaissance and Manueline architecture, but also one of Portugal's most potent national symbols. A monument to the country's maritime triumphs across the centuries, it was built between 1515 and 1520 by Francisco de Arruda, a Portuguese architect who had previously worked on a variety of military projects in Morocco. His travels in North Africa made a lasting impression on him, and this is reflected in the use of a wide range of Moorish motifs on the tower. Chief of these are the little domes crowning the

The tower's projecting bastion (left); stone balcony on the elevation of the tower (middle); looking like the ultimate fairy-tale castle, the tower was built to defend Lisbon's port and was the place to keep a wary eye out for pirates coming up the River Tejo (right)

battlements, and the jutting corner sentry boxes, which are combined with arcaded windows and delicate Venetian-style loggias.

Changing roles Once the tower stood proudly out in the river, acting as a defensive bastion guarding the Restelo, or port, from pirates. Today the Tejo's ever-changing course has left it stranded on the shore. Up close, you can make out the cross motif adorning every battlement. This was the symbol of the Order of Christ, the successor to the Knights Templar in Portugal. A jutting bastion leads to a small internal cloister, below which are rudimentary storerooms and dungeons. The breezy second-level terrace—which gives good views—features an intricately carved statue of the Madonna (Our Lady of the Safe Homecoming). Steps lead up to the top of the tower for more views.

THE BASICS

www.mosteirojeronimas.pt
b4
Avenida de Brasília
213 620 034
May–end Sep Tue–Sun 10–6.30; Oct–end Apr Tue–Sun 10–5. Closed Mon and public hols
28, 714, 727, 729, 751; tram 15
Belém (Cascais line) from Cais do Sodré
Poor
Moderate, free Sun until 2pm

More to See

CENTRO CULTURAL DE BELÉM

www.ccb.pt

You can easily while away a few hours at this dynamic public art and performance space, known as the CCB. The hugh, stark block, with sweeping clean lines and lovely terraces overlooking the water, was built in 1992 and is the creation of Vittorio Gregotti and Manuel Salgado.

c3 Praça do Império 213 612 400 Mon–Fri 8–8, Sat–Sun 10–7; evening performances vary Café Belém 28, 714, 727, 729, 751; tram 15 Free; charge for exhibitions and performances

MUSEU NACIONAL DE ARQUEOLÓGIA

www.mnarqueologia-ipmuseus.pt

You might consider this rambling archaeological museum, founded in 1893, a little threadbare in places, but there are plenty of fascinating objects, from widely differing epochs of Portuguese history, to make a visit worthwhile.

c3 Praça do Império 213 620 000 Tue–Sun 10–6. Closed public hols Belém 28, 714, 727, 729, 751; tram 15 Moderate, free Sun until 2pm

MUSEU PRESIDÊNCIA DA REPÚBLICA

www.museu.presidencia.pt

At the President's official residence, this museum brings the President closer to his citizens. Using innovative interactive displays, you can learn about the institution and its history.

d3 Praça Afonso de Albuquerque 213 614 660 Museum: Tue–Sun 10–6; Palace: Sat 10–5 Belém 28, 714, 727, 729, 751; tram 15 Museum only: inexpensive; Museum and Palace: moderate

PLANETÁRIO CALOUSTE GULBENKIAN

www.planetario.online.pt

Sponsored by the Gulbenkian Foundation, the Planetarium is in an annex of the Museu de Marinha, and incorporates special children's shows.

c3 Praça do Império 213 620 002 Wed–Thu 4pm, Sat–Sun 11 and 3.30pm Belém 28, 714, 727, 729, 751; tram 15 Moderate

Reach for the stars at the Planetarium

PAPIRO
AZULE

Restaurants

PRICES

Prices are approximate, based on a 3-course meal for one person.

€€€	over €25
€€	€15–€25
€	under €15

ANTIGA CASA DOS PASTÉIS DE BELÉM (€)

www.pasteisdebelem.pt

This old café and pastry shop in Belém is renow-ned for its cakes, particularly the distinctive *pastéis* de Belém, tiny flaky tarts filled with custard.

d1 Rua de Belém 84–92 213 637 423 May–Oct daily 8am–12am; Nov–Apr Mon–Sat 8am–11pm, Sun 8am–10pm 28, 727, 729, 751; tram 15

BBC (€€€)

www.belembarcafe.com

Dine indoors or out in chic surroundings with superb views over the River Tejo. The Belém Bar Café's Portuguese cuisine is very popular. Often live music.

c4 Avenida Brasília, Pavilhão Poente 213 624 232 Tue–Fri lunch, dinner, Sat dinner only 28, 727, 729, 751; tram 15

CAIS DE BELÉM (€€)

An outside terrace makes excellent use of an esplanade over-looking the park. You can expect good plates of Portuguese regional cooking here.

d3 Rua Vieira Portuense 64 213 621 537 Thu–Tue lunch, dinner 28, 727, 729, 751; tram 15

MERCADO DO PEIXE (€€€)

www.mercadodopeixe.web.pt

One of Lisbon's more upmarket fish and seafood restaurants, it is well worth the trip out to Ajuda (just before Belém) to sample some of the best seafood in the city.

d1 Estrada Pedro Teixeira 213 616 070 Tue–Sat lunch, dinner, Sun lunch only 727, 729; tram 18

CHARGES AND TIPS

Restaurants will often bring plates of starters such as bread, ham, cheeses and olives. These will be charged to your bill as *couvert*, or cover charge, unless you send them back. Very few people do this as they are great and unless you are in a very fancy restaurant they will make little difference to the final bill. Value-added tax, or IVA, is added to restaurant bills at 8 per cent. Most bills say *IVA incluido* and already include this charge. Tips are welcomed and generally expected as a service charge is rarely included on the bill. Anything from 5 per cent is considered acceptable.

O CARVOEIRO (€€)

Overlooking the park, this unpretentious restaurant attracts tourists and locals alike to sample simple meat and fish dishes cooked to perfection. The sardines are excellent and the portions are huge.

d3 Rua Vieira Portuense 66–68 213 637 998 Tue–Sat lunch, dinner, Sun lunch only 28, 727, 729, 751; tram 15

O CASEIRO (€€-€€€)

Locals flock to this simple Portuguese restaurant, which serves generous portions of good uncom-plicated food. There are vaulted ceilings and walls hung with air-cured hams and pumpkins.

d3 Rua de Belém 35 213 638 803 Mon–Sat lunch, dinner; closed Aug 28, 727, 729, 751; tram 15

VELA LATINA (€€€)

www.velalatina.pt

This tastefully decorated restaurant has one of Lisbon's prime locations, on the waterfront beside the Torre de Belém. Don't get the restaurant confused with the popular self-service restaurant at the front of the complex. The chef mixes national and international cuisine.

b4 Doca Bom Sucesso 213 017 118 Mon–Sat lunch, dinner 28, 727, 729, 751; tram 15

Just a few bus or metro stops away and you are in the city's suburbs, where you'll discover a plethora of other attractions to keep you busy for a long time.

Sights	100–105
Excursions	106

Top 25 TOP 25

Igreja da Madre de Deus ⊳ **100**

Museu Nacional do Azulejo ⊳ **102**

Parque das Nações ⊳ **103**

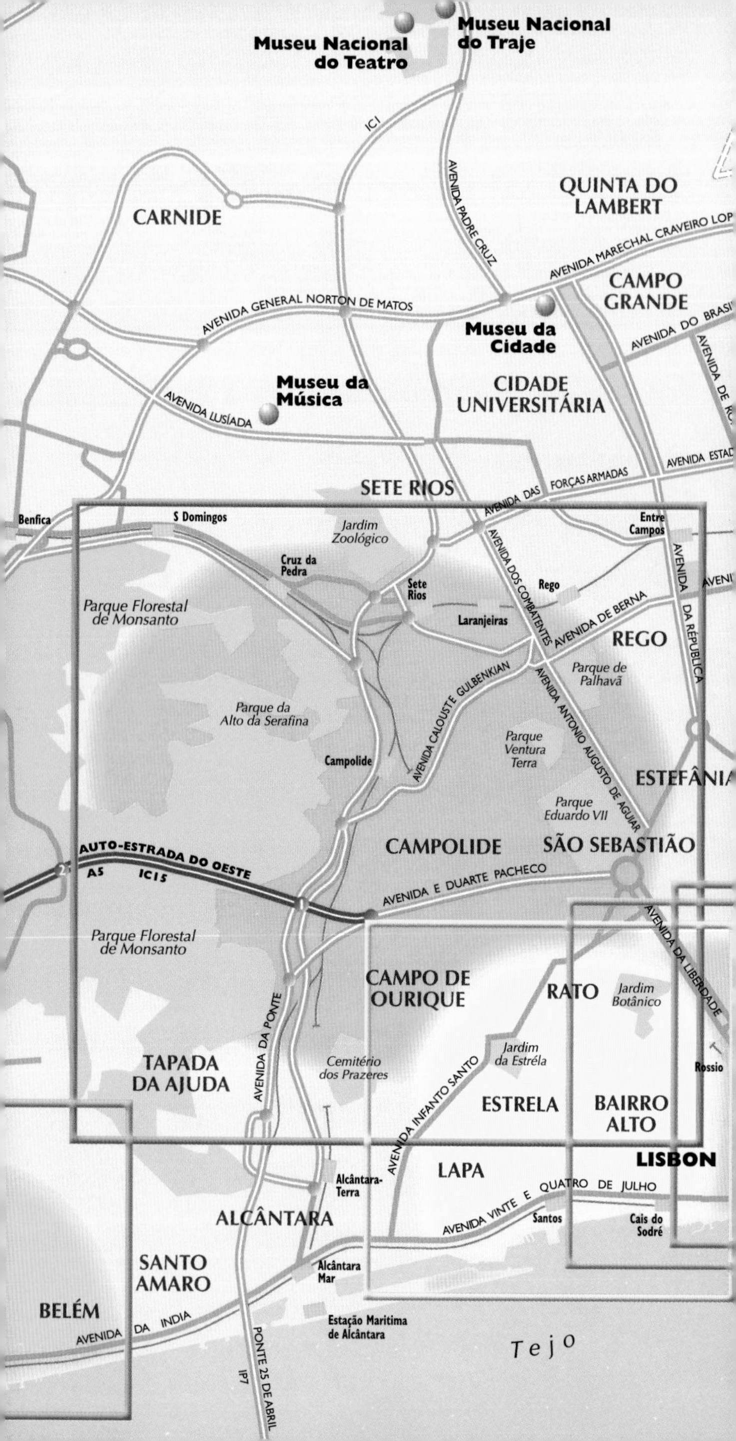

Museu Nacional do Traje
Museu Nacional do Teatro
IC1
AVENIDA PADRE CRUZ
QUINTA DO LAMBERT
CARNIDE
AVENIDA MARECHAL CRAVEIRO LOP
CAMPO GRANDE
AVENIDA GENERAL NORTON DE MATOS
Museu da Cidade
AVENIDA DO BRASI
Museu da Música
CIDADE UNIVERSITÁRIA
AVENIDA LUSÍADA
SETE RIOS
AVENIDA DAS FORÇAS ARMADAS
AVENIDA ESTAD
Benfica
S Domingos
Jardim Zoológico
Entre Campos
Cruz da Pedra
Sete Rios
Rego
Parque Florestal de Monsanto
Laranjeiras
AVENIDA DOS COMBATENTES
AVENIDA DE BERNA
REGO
AVENIDA DA REPÚBLICA
AVENIDA CALOUSTE GULBENKIAN
Parque de Palhavã
Parque da Alto da Serafina
AVENIDA ANTONIO AUGUSTO DE AGUIAR
Parque Ventura Terra
Campolide
ESTEFÂNIA
Parque Eduardo VII
CAMPOLIDE
SÃO SEBASTIÃO
AUTO-ESTRADA DO OESTE
A5
IC15
AVENIDA E DUARTE PACHECO
AVENIDA DA LIBERDADE
Parque Florestal de Monsanto
CAMPO DE OURIQUE
RATO
Jardim Botânico
Jardim da Estréla
Rossio
Cemitério dos Prazeres
AVENIDA INFANTO SANTO
TAPADA DA AJUDA
AVENIDA DA PONTE
ESTRELA
BAIRRO ALTO
LISBON
LAPA
Alcântara-Terra
AVENIDA VINTE E QUATRO DE JULHO
ALCÂNTARA
Santos
Cais do Sodré
SANTO AMARO
Alcântara Mar
BELÉM
Estação Maritima de Alcântara
AVENIDA DA INDIA
Tejo
PONTE 25 DE ABRIL
IP7

Aeroporto da Portela de Sacavem
Aeroporto de Lisboa
IP1
AVENIDA DE BERLIM
IC17
AVENIDA INFANTE DOM HENRIQUE
Parque das Nações
Olivais
OLIVAIS SUL
Oceanário
Pavilhão do Conhecimento-Ciência Viva
AVENIDA MARECHAL GOMES DA COSTA
AVENIDA DO SANTO CONDESTÁVEL
AVENIDA ALMIRANTE GAGO COUTINHO
Parque da Mata de Alvalade
TERESINHAS
ALVALADE
Parque Vale Fundão
BRAÇO DE PRATA
Parque da Bela Vista
AREEIRO
Areeiro
CHELAS
Braço de Prata
OLAIAS
Marvila
Chelas
ALTO DO PINA
PICHELEIRA
Cemitério do Alto de São João
AVENIDA MOUZINHO DE ALBUQUERQUE
AVENIDA ALMIRANTE REIS
BAIRRO LOPES
Museu Nacional do Azulejo
Igreja da Madre de Deus
AVENIDA INFANTE DOM HENRIQUE
RUE DA PALMA
GRAÇA
Santa Apolónia
ALFAMA
Tejo
0
1 km
0
1 mile

Igreja da Madre de Deus

HIGHLIGHTS

- Manueline doorway
- Gilt woodwork
- Vault paintings
- Wall paintings
- Chapter house
- Sacristy
- Capela de Santo António
- Crypt

TIP

- Combining a visit here with one to the Museu Nacional do Azulejo (▷ 102) makes an enticing double bill.

This church has some of the city's most opulent decoration. Its lavish gilt baroque pulpit and altar, and walls covered with tiles and 16th–17th-century paintings, make it a place that should be on every visitor's agenda.

Humble beginnings Like Belém to the west, this grand and sumptuously decorated church, some 3km (1.5 miles) east of the Baixa, is one of the many sights in Lisbon worth leaving the heart of the city to see. Originally part of a larger convent, it was founded in 1509 by Dona Leonor, widow of Dom João II. Later it was expanded by João III, only to be virtually destroyed during the 1755 earthquake. Subsequent rebuilding turned the church's interior into one of the most magnificent in the city, but the exterior's Manueline

A riot of golden opulence enhances the main altar of the church (left); paintings displayed in gilded frames and artwork created from azulejos *(right)*

doorway and the crypt (with a grandiose altar and 16th-century Seville tiles) have survived from Leonor's earlier foundation.

Elaborate church The interior is a masterpiece of decorative excess, laden with gilt, wood and tiles and decorated with several glorious paintings. Scenes from the Life of the Virgin fill the coffered main vault, paintings high on the walls depict scenes from the Life of St. Francis (right wall when facing the altar) and the Life of St. Clare (left wall when facing altar). The lower walls are covered in beautiful blue-and-white 18th-century Dutch tiles. In the even more breathtaking chapter house, virtually every surface is adorned with tiles or gilt-framed paintings. Also make a point of seeing the Capela de Santo António and the sacristy, which are similarly embellished.

THE BASICS

- Off map at M5
- Rua da Madre de Deus 4
- 218 100 340
- Wed–Sun 10–6, Tue 2–6
- Arroios, then bus 794
- 718, 742
- Poor
- Free

Museu Nacional do Azulejo

Behind the gates, the Museu Nacional do Azulejo conceals superb tiled artworks

THE BASICS

www.mnazulejo-ipmuseus.pt
Off map at M5
Rua da Madre de Deus 4
218 100 340
Wed–Sun 10–6, Tue 2–6
Café
Arriois, then bus 794
718, 742, 794
Poor
Inexpensive. Free on Sun and public hols until 2

HIGHLIGHTS

- Tiled Manueline cloisters
- Lisbon cityscape (1738)
- Tiled Nativity (1580)
- Tiled battle scenes
- The Hunting Room, with a distinctive Far Eastern theme

This lovely museum, in the tranquil Igreja da Madre de Deus (▷ 100–101), traces the history of tile-making. Through Dutch, Moorish and Hispanic influences, here you'll see the Portuguese emerge as masters of their craft.

Simple and sophisticated The museum's earliest *azulejos* (a corruption of the Arabic word *azraq*—azure—or *zalayja*, meaning a smooth stone or polished terracotta) date from the beginning of the 16th century. Later exhibits show how simple, single-hued designs gave way to more sophisticated patterning allowed by the new majolica techniques imported from Italy. As the art developed, *azulejos* became still more complex and vibrant. Later still, they were influenced by the single-motif patterns of Dutch tiles and by the fashion for blue and white inspired by the arrival of Ming dynasty porcelain in Europe. Simpler designs also resulted from the 1755 earthquake, when large numbers of cheap decorative tiles were required for rebuilding.

Museum highlights The museum is full of beautiful examples. Look for the 38m (125ft) tiled cityscape of Lisbon, made in 1738 prior to the 1755 earthquake, and the small Manueline cloister decorated with its original 16th- and 17th-century tiles. Also, don't miss the fine, 16th-century polychrome tile picture of Nossa Senhora da Vida, a nativity scene. There are delightful 18th-century blue-and-white tile scenes of everyday life, such as a doctor giving an injection.

The modern face of Lisbon–the Parque das Nações (left) featuring the Oceanário (right)

Parque das Nações

In contrast to historic Lisbon's steep hills and narrow streets, this stretch of futuristic waterfront development is where you will discover the face of the 21st-century city, set among wide promenades and waterside gardens.

Background This former industrial wasteland, which until the early 1990s few *Lisboetas* set foot on, was chosen as the site for Lisbon's Expo 1998. It has subsequently become a thriving urban district, the Parque das Nações.

Getting started As soon as you arrive at the iconic Gare do Oriente station it is obvious you are stepping into the 21st century. You pass straight into the Vasco da Gama shopping mall–Lisbon's biggest shopping and leisure complex, occupying four floors. Pick up a plan of the Parque at the information desk. If you want transport take the miniature train around the Parque.

What to do The area contains two of Lisbon's largest concert venues, a casino, hotels and a plethora of eating and drinking options, plus major attractions such as the Oceanário (▷ 105) and the Pavilhão do Conhecimento–Ciência Viva (▷ 105). There are also play areas and bike rental. Take the cable car (Teleférico) from the waterfront and enjoy a bird's-eye view of the complete site. At the north end is the Torre Vasco da Gama, built as a symbol of the great 15th-century voyager (closed to visitors). Don't miss a stroll among the waterfront gardens.

THE BASICS

www.portaldasnacoes.pt

Off map to north

Alameda dos Oceanos

218 919 333; cable car 218 956 143; shopping mall 218 930 600

Cable car: Jul–end Sep daily 11–8 (10–8 at weekends and public holidays); Oct–end Jun daily 11–7 (10–7 at weekends and public holidays). Shopping mall: daily 10–midnight

Restaurants and cafés

Oriente

Cable car: moderate. Prices for Oceanário and Pavilhão do Conhecimento–Ciência Viva (▷ 105). Inclusive ticket *Cartão do Parque* for all main sights: expensive

HIGHLIGHTS

- **Oceanário**
- **Teleférico (cable car)**
- **Pavilhão do Conhecimento–Ciência Viva**
- **Vasco de Gama mall**
- **Waterside gardens**

More to See

MUSEU DA CIDADE

The Museum of the City lies north of the heart of the city in the northwest corner of the Campo Grande. A stimulating museum in a lovely setting, it uses paintings, prints and drawings to trace the development of Lisbon through the centuries. Highlights include a model of pre-earthquake Lisbon, a 17th-century painting showing the Praça do Comércio before the Marqués de Pombal renovated it, and a picture of the poet Fernando Pessoa, painted in 1954, 19 years after his death.

Off map at F1 Campo Grande 245 217 513 200 Tue–Sun 10–1, 2–6 Campo Grande 7, 36, 47, 750 Inexpensive; free on Sun

MUSEU DA MÚSICA

www.museudamusica-ipmuseus.pt

A collection of musical instruments from around Europe, dating from the 16th to 21st centuries.

Off map at E1 Rua João Freitas Branco 217 710 990 Tue–Sat 10–6 Alto dos Moinhos Inexpensive. Under 14s free

MUSEU NACIONAL DO TEATRO

www.museudoteatro-ipmuseus.pt

The National Theatre Museum concentrates on the personalities who have graced the Lisbon stage over the years, which makes it of limited interest to the foreign visitor. It is worth a look if you are visiting the area's Costume Museum (▷ 104), though, as it also has theatrical costumes, props, photographs, stage designs and other theatrical ephemera.

Off map at F1 Parque de Monteiro-Mor, Estrada do Lumiar 10 217 567 410 Wed–Sun 10–6, Tue 2–6 (closes at 5 in winter). Closed public hols Lumiar 7, 36, 108 Moderate; joint ticket with Museu Nacional do Traje. Free Sun until 2pm

MUSEU NACIONAL DO TRAJE

www.museudotraje-impmuseus.pt

The National Museum of Costume occupies the tiled and frescoed Palácio do Duque de Palmela, also known as the Palácio Monteiro-Mor, in the Parque do Monteiro-Mor at Lumiar. Visit the Jardim Botânico, dotted with pools, plants and trees in a rugged hilly

The National Theatre Museum set in the lush Parque de Monteiro-Mór

setting, as well as the museum itself, which has beautiful old tapestries, jewels, toys and costumes.

Off map at F1 Parque de Monteiro-Mor, Largo Júlio de Castilho, Lumiar 217 590 318 Tue–Sun 10–6 (closes at 5 in winter) Lumiar 7, 36, 108 Moderate; joint ticket with Museu Nacional do Teatro. Free Sun until 2pm

OCEANÁRIO

www.oceanario.pt

Spectacularly designed by Peter Chermayeff, this is one of Europe's largest oceanariums. Opened in 1998, as part of Expo 98, it has species from the five different oceans. The vast central tank, Global Ocean, is surrounded by four smaller tanks with two viewing levels. You'll encounter sharks, manta, barracudas, ocean sunfish, rays and giant groupers. Begin on the upper level, passing through different climatic zones—the puffins, penguins and otters are the draw here. Move down to the lower level to discover an underwater environment. Additional smaller tanks enclose such wonders as living coral reefs, mangrove forests and Australian dragon fish—their camouflage so impressive it is almost impossible to detect them against the weeds.

Off map to north Esplanada Dom Carlos I, Doca dos Olivais, Parque das Nações 218 917 002 Apr–end Oct daily 10–7; Nov–end Mar daily 10–6 Oriente Expensive

PAVILHÃO DO CONHECIMENTO —CIÊNCIA VIVA

www.pavconhecimento.pt

A science and technology museum that stimulates scientific enquiry using experimental methods and exploration. Through exhibitions and dozens of interactive activities, visitors can discover science in a relaxed and enjoyable way. There is a shop where you can buy science-related gifts to follow up your day of discovery.

Off map to north Alameda dos Oceanos, Parque das Nações 218 917 100 Tue–Fri 10–6, Sat, Sun 11–7 Oriente Expensive

Some of the 7,000 or so costumes exhibited at the National Museum of Costume

Watch out! There are sharks about in the Oceanário

Excursions

THE BASICS

www.cm-mafra.pt
Distance: 40km (25 miles)
Journey Time: 50 min
Empresa Mafrense buses depart hourly from Campo Grande bus terminal, Lisbon

Palácio-Convento
Torreão Sul, Terreiro Dom João V 261 810 550 Wed–Mon 10–5; last tour 4.30
Moderate

MAFRA

The little town of Mafra is dominated by the monumental Palácio-Convento, one of the largest baroque monasteries and palaces in Europe.

Begun in 1717, the Palácio was built by Dom João V, who had pledged to build a monastery should he and his wife have a child. Bárbara, the future Queen of Spain, was born within a year. Finance for the project was provided by the gold and diamonds of Brazil. The plan was for a monastery of 13 monks—in the end it housed 300. Around 50,000 workers and 7,000 soldiers toiled on the building, a huge folly of 880 rooms. Today you can visit the rather chilly church and rooms.

THE BASICS

www.cm-sintra.pt
Distance: 25km (16 miles)
Journey Time: 40 min
From Lisbon's Rossio or Sete Rios, every 20 min
Praça da República 23
219 231 157

SINTRA

Sintra is a town of splendid royal palaces and beautiful scenery. The sights are not within walking distance, so you will need to use the efficient bus service, taxis or a car, or join an organized tour.

In Sintra-Vila (the town itself) the main thing to see is the Palácio Nacional, begun by Dom João I in the 15th century and used as a royal palace until the end of the 19th century. Just south of Sintra-Vila lies the Castelo dos Mouros, a Moorish castle begun in the 8th century. The views from its rocky pinnacles are magnificent. Farther south, around 3km (1.8 miles) from Sintra-Vila, lies another royal palace, the Palácio da Pena, a wonderfully pretentious monument built in the 19th century. A madcap medieval pastiche, its exterior is all battlements and towers. Its park and gardens are delightful, and the views from its terraces sublime. The recently restored Quinta da Regaleira, just to the east of Sintra, is one of the finest examples of late 19th-century revivalist art, with its masonic 'well of initiation', gargoyles, mythological grottos and neo-Manueline palace and chapel.

Ranging from luxurious converted palaces and modern upmarket hotels to simple *residências* and *pensões*, Lisbon has accommodation to suit everyone.

Introduction **108**

Budget Hotels **109**

Mid-Range Hotels **110–111**

Luxury Hotels **112**

Introduction

If you like to stay where it's all happening, the Baixa and Chiado areas are the places to be, but for something more peaceful and still close to the action, choose a hotel on or around Avenida da Liberdade. In the Alfama district you will find *pensões* still living in the past, while some of Lisbon's best hotels, housed in elegant historic buildings, are in the prosperous suburb of Lapa.

Getting the Best Price

Bear in mind rates vary according to season and will soar in peak periods (by as much as 40 per cent). Hotels often quote their most expensive rates, but don't be afraid to ask if they have a less expensive room. Agree the price before you make your reservation, and ask for written confirmation if you're booking ahead. In Portugal hotels and *pensões* are legally required to post the room rates on the back of the bedroom door, which should include IVA (VAT). If you have a child with you, most hotels will put an extra bed in the room for a small charge.

What to Expect

As in most major European cities, Portugal's hotels are graded between one and five stars, the facilities, service and comfort reflected in the price and rating. *Pensões* and *residências* are a good budget option; their main distinction being that *residências* are unlikely to serve meals other than breakfast. These are classified, from one to three stars—a three-star *pensão* would cost about the same as a one-star hotel.

BOOKING ONLINE

When you are ready to book your accommodation, it's worth checking out some internet sites first to get a good price on the hotel you have chosen to stay at. Reputable sites include www.laterooms.com, www.expedia.com and www.lastminute.com, but there are many others providing the same service. If you want to go self-catering, take a look at www.holiday-rentals.co.uk or www.ownersdirect.co.uk, who list a variety of options. Many Lisbon hotels have their own websites with an online booking service.

Budget Hotels

PRICES

Expect to pay under €100 per night for a double room in a budget hotel.

HOTEL BORGES

www.hotelborges.com

A comfortable if unexceptional hotel worth staying at as it is close to the Chiado shopping district. Popular, so book ahead.

J8 Rua Garrett 108–110 213 461 951; fax 213 426 617 Baixa-Chiado Tram 28

PENSÃO GALIZIA

On the fourth floor of a block between the Baixa and Chiado districts. Although all the rooms are smallish, some do have balconies.

K8 Rua do Crucifixio 50–4° 213 428 430 Baixa-Chiado

PENSÃO LONDRES

www.pensaolondres.com.pt

This friendly and efficient pension in an old townhouse is plusher than most in its price category. Rooms vary considerably; some on the fourth floor have views, so look first.

H7 Rua Dom Pedro V 53 213 462 203; fax 213 465 682 758, 773, 790

PENSÃO RESIDENCIAL ROYAL

Possibly one of the best deals in central Lisbon, this small residencial in the Baixa offers clean, freshly decorated rooms with en-suites. Don't be put off by the shabby exterior.

K8 Rua do Crucifixo 50-3° 213 479 006 Baixa-Chiado

PENSÃO SÃO JOÃO DE PRAÇA

An amiable pension in a pleasant Alfama townhouse near the cathedral. Rooms are clean.

L8 Rua São João da Praça 97–2° 218 862 591; fax 218 880 415 37; tram 12, 28

POUSADA DE JUVENTUDE DE LISBOA

www.pousadasjuventude.pt

Lisbon's 176-bed youth hostel has private double rooms as well as dormitory accommodation. The hostel is open all day, and there is no curfew.

H4 Rua Andrade Corvo 46 213 532 696; fax 213 537 541 Picoas 727, 738, 745

USEFUL TIPS

If you are searching for inexpensive accommodation remember that many pensions are in buildings that look much more run down from the outside than they are inside. Many cheaper places are on the upper floors of blocks, so note the address carefully. In Lisbon a street number is often followed by the floor number: 74-3°, for example, means the property is at number 74 in the street and on the third floor.

RESIDENCIAL AVENIDA PARQUE

www.avenidaparque.com

A great-value *residência* overlooking the Parque Eduardo VII. An elegant wooden staircase leads up to rooms with modern furniture and coordinated soft furnishings; some with balconies. Some rooms sleep 2, 3, or 4—useful for families.

H4 Avenida Sidónio Pais 6 218 532 181 Parque

RESIDENCIAL CAMÕES

www.pensaoresidencialcamoes.com

A perfect location in the Bairro Alto is the main selling point of this friendly first-floor *residência*. Small, attractive rooms and nice communal areas. More expensive rooms have balconies and/or private bathrooms.

J7 Travessa do Poço da Cidade 38–1° 213 467 510; fax 213 464 048 Rossio, Baixa-Chiado 758

SÉ GUESTHOUSE

This welcoming guesthouse is in the same pleasant and well-located townhouse as the Pensão São João da Praça (▷ above). Bathrooms are shared, but the light and airy rooms are a touch smarter than its near neighbour, and all have TVs. A good breakfast is included in the room rate.

L8 Rua São João da Praça 97–1° 218 864 400 37; tram 12, 28

Mid-Range Hotels

PRICES

Expect to pay between €100 and €250 per night for a double room in a mid-range hotel.

AS JANELAS VERDES

www.heritage.pt

An intimate hotel in an 18th-century townhouse with spacious and sumptuously fitted rooms. The location means the front rooms can be noisy.

F9 Rua das Janelas Verdes 47 213 968 143; fax 213 968 144 Santos (from Cais do Sodré) 60, 727; tram 25

BRITÂNIA

www.heritage.pt

A traditional hotel built in 1944 on a pleasant street just east of the Avenida da Liberdade. The hotel retains an old-fashioned charm and its art deco interior. Courteous service. Breakfast is the only meal served.

H5 Rua Rodrigues Sampaio 17 213 155 016; fax 213 155 021 Avenida 44, 711, 732, 745, all services to Avenida da Liberdade

CASA DE SÃO MAMEDE

www.saomamede.web.pt

This homely and pleasantly traditional pension is by the Jardim Botânico (▷ 64) on the northern fringes of the Bairro Alto. The 28 rooms are simple, but pleasantly furnished.

H6 Rua da Escola Politécnica 159 213 963 166; fax 213 951 896 Rato 758

EXECUTIVE

www.sanahotels.com

Modern hotel but small and very attractively fitted out. It is close to the Gulbenkian—not central but with good transport to central Lisbon. There is no restaurant but breakfast is served.

H2 Avenida Conde de Valbom 56–62 217 951 157; fax 217 951 166 São Sebastião 16, 36, 726, 746

HERITAGE AV LIBERDADE

www.heritage.pt

The lovely deep blue façade draws your attention to this small boutique hotel, opened in 2006. Housed in a restored late-18th-century building in the heart of the city, the interior combines stylish modern design with traditional Portugal. 40 bedrooms.

J6 Avenida da Liberdade 28 213 404 040; fax 213 404 044 Avenida All services to Avenida da Liberdade

HOTEL JORGE V

www.hoteljorgev.com

This 1960s building is just off the Avenida da Liberdade, close to the heart of the city. Small rooms but nice balconies for breakfast and tea.

H5 Rua Mouzinho da Silveira 3 213 562 525; fax 213 150 319 Marquês de Pombal All services to Avenida da Liberdade

LAWRENCE'S

www.lawrenceshotel.com

Claiming to be Iberia's oldest inn, Lawrence's offers individually decorated rooms, personalized service and a fantastic restaurant.

Off map Rua Consigliéri Pedroso 38–40 219 105 500 Sintra from Rossio

LISBOA REGENCY CHIADO

www.regency-hotels-resorts.com

A boutique hotel in the heart of the city's smartest shopping district, with great views of the

WHERE TO STAY

Of the more expensive hotels, the older ones tend to be close to the Rossio, while the newer establishments are in the north on, or just off, the Avenida da Liberdade. Other choice hotels are in residential suburbs well away from the heart of the city, mostly in the west or northeast. Most budget options are near the Rossio and in the Baixa, but these central locations are likely to be noisy unless you can secure an off-street room. Two of the city's most picturesque places to stay, the atmospheric Bairro Alto and Alfama districts, have relatively few hotels.

Castelo. The bedrooms are a mix of Portuguese and oriental design and all have modern facilities. You can enjoy an excellent breakfast while gazing over the rooftops through the bay windows.
K8 Rua Nova do Almada 114 213 256 100; fax 213 256 161 Baixa-Chiado 758

MÉTROPOLE

www.almeidahotels.com
An imposing and elegant building in the Rossio—central but consequently also noisy. The air-conditioning and double-glazing help.
K7 Praça Dom Pedro IV 30 213 219 030; fax 213 469 166 Rossio

MIRAPARQUE

www.miraparque.com
An almost perfect mid-range friendly hotel on a quiet tree-lined street overlooking the Parque Eduardo VII and Pavilhão dos Desportos. Rooms are a little dated, but large, bright and spotlessly clean. Serves good Portuguese food. Only a minute from the metro.
H4 Avenida Sidónio Pais 12 213 524 286; fax 213 578 920 Parque

MUNDIAL

www.hotel-mundial.pt
A large hotel that first opened in 1958, which has been thoroughly refurbished over the years. The 373 modern bedrooms are a good size and have big picture windows giving good light. Situated in the heart of Lisbon close to Rossio and within easy walking distance of many restaurants and attractions.
K7 Praça Martim Moniz 2 218 842 000; fax 218 842 110 Rossio

SENHORA DO MONTE

www.maisturismo.pt/sramonte
This lovely hilltop hotel in the Graça district, north of the Castelo, would be the first choice in its category if it were closer to the inner city. It has 28 attractive rooms, some with balconies and air-conditioning, and a relaxed and amiable ambience. No restaurant, but breakfast is served.
L6 Calçada do Monte 39 218 866 002; fax 218 877 783 Martim Moniz 40, 708; tram 12, 28

NOISE

Lisbon is notoriously noisy. Expensive hotels are not immune to the cacophony, but most have double-glazing and air-conditioning, which provide a measure of protection. Cheaper hotels are usually not so blessed, and may be near the Rossio, Baixa or Bairro Alto, three of the city's busier districts. Try to avoid rooms on the street, and check for bars or restaurants nearby, which are likely to be open until the small hours.

SOLAR DOS MOUROS

www.solardosmouros.pt
This small unique hotel in the Alfama district is ideal for romantic art lovers. The 12 individual bedrooms—including a duplex suite—are decorated with African art and wonderful abstract pieces by owner-painter Luís Lemos. All rooms have a lovely view either over the castle or the river.
L7 Rua do Milagre de Santo António 6 218 854 940 Tram 28

VIP INN VENEZA

www.viphotels.com
This palatial townhouse, built in 1886 by a wealthy lawyer, offers excellent value for money. A vibrant mural of Lisbon adorns the grand staircase that leads to 32 modest but spacious and well-equipped bedrooms. A very efficient hotel with accommodating staff.
J6 Avenida da Liberdade 189 213 522 618; fax 213 526 678 Avenida All services to Avenida da Liberdade

YORK HOUSE

www.yorkhouselisboa.com
Although York House is west of the heart of the city, it is one of Lisbon's most popular hotels, with a lovely tree- and plant-filled courtyard, and 34 simple but tasteful rooms.
F9 Rua das Janelas 32 213 962 435; fax 213 972 793 Santos 60, 727; tram 25

Luxury Hotels

PRICES

Expect to pay over €250 per night for a double room at a luxury hotel.

AVENIDA PALACE

www.hotelavenidapalace.pt

A traditional hotel at the heart of the city. Built in 1842, it lies between the busy Rossio and Praça dos Restauradores, but the rooms away from the street are calm, comfortable and spacious. Be sure to check internet rates for good reductions.

J7 Rua 1 de Dezembro 123 213 218 100; fax 213 422 884 Rossio

BAIRRO ALTO HOTEL

www.bairroaltohotel.com

A fusion of old and new in the fashionable Bairro Alto quarter, with 55 rooms in a chic contemporary style. The peaceful rooftop terrace gives panoramic views over the city.

J8 Praça Luís de Camões 2 213 408 288; fax 213 408 299 Baixa-Chiado 758

LAPA PALACE

www.lapapalace.com

This 94-room five-star hotel is one of Lisbon's most expensive. It is in a 19th-century palace and a modern six-floor block with luxurious rooms. Lovely garden with pool.

E8 Rua do Pau de Bandeira 4 213 949 494; fax 213 950 665 Santos 713; tram 25

PALÁCIO DE BELMONTE

www.palaciobelmonte.com

This beautiful 16th-century palace in the Alfama district has been painstakingly restored to make it one of the world's finest luxury hotels, and one of the most discreet. State-of-the-art comfort combines with sheer elegance in the 11 individual suites, which are decorated with 18th-century *azulejos* and rich hues and have amazing views. The peaceful terraces and gardens are around a black marble pool.

L8 Páteo Dom Fradique 14 218 816 600; fax 218 816 609 Tram 28

PALÁCIO DE SETEAIS

www.tivolihotels.com

A sumptuous 30-room hotel in a lovely 19th-century palace, with period furnishings. The views are all that you could wish of Sintra.

Off map Rua Barbosa do Bocage 10, 2710 Sintra 219 233 200; fax 219 234 277 Sintra

RESERVATIONS

Book a room well in advance if you plan to visit Lisbon over Easter or during midsummer. At other times it is safest to book, but some sort of accommodation can usually be found on arrival. The information desk at the main Portela Airport has details of day-to-day availability but cannot make bookings for you. The city's main tourist offices will also supply lists of accommodation.

PESTANA PALACE

www.pestana.com

This beautiful yellow 19th-century palace set in wonderful grounds may be a little way out, but it is perfect for an indulgent break relaxing by the pool in opulent surroundings. The 173 rooms and 17 suites are amazing and the restaurant is superb.

Off map Rua Jaú 54, Ajuda 213 615 600; fax 213 615 601 738, 742; tram 18

RITZ FOUR SEASONS

www.fourseasons.com

Lisbon's most famous deluxe hotel since it opened in the 1950s. All 310 rooms have their own balconies. Swimming pool, fitness and spa facilities, and also on-site car parking.

G5 Rua Rodrigo do Fonseca 88 213 811 400; fax 213 831 783 Marquês de Pombal 12, 48, 53, 83, 702, 711, 713, 723

SOFITEL LISBOA

www.sofitel.com

One of the city's newest luxury options, with 163 rooms, this hotel is stylish and modern and appeals to business people as well as tourists.

J6 Avenida da Liberdade 127 213 228 300; fax 213 228 310 Avenida All services to Avenida da Liberdade

Lisbon's bus and metro service is excellent, but it is often best to get around on foot, making use of the odd tram trundling up the steep cobbled streets or elevator to whisk you to the top of the hill.

Planning Ahead	**114–115**
Getting There	**116–117**
Getting Around	**118–119**
Essential Facts	**120–121**
Language	**122–123**
Timeline	**124–125**

Planning Ahead

When to Go

Lisbon's hottest and busiest months are July and August; many of the city's inhabitants take their holiday then so some shops and restaurants may be shut. The best months to visit are April, May, June, September and October, when the city is less busy and the weather is mild.

TIME

Portugal observes the same time as Britain, 5 hours ahead of New York, 8 hours ahead of Los Angeles.

AVERAGE DAILY MAXIMUM TEMPERATURES

JAN	FEB	MAR	APR	MAY	JUN	JUL	AUG	SEP	OCT	NOV	DEC
57°F	59°F	63°F	67°F	71°F	77°F	81°F	82°F	79°F	72°F	63°F	58°F
14°C	15°C	17°C	20°C	21°C	25°C	27°C	28°C	26°C	22°C	17°C	15°C

Spring (March–May): Often mild and sunny. Rainfall is often high in March but usually decreases quickly in April and May.
Summer (June–September): Hot and dry, but temperatures are tempered by cooling sea breezes. Rain is rare in July and August, but there may be thunderstorms.
Autumn (October–November): Temperatures remain good, with many balmy days, and often clear skies, but rain picks up in October and November.
Winter (December–February): Lisbon bears the brunt of wet Atlantic depressions and rainfall is highest in December and January, with February a little drier.

WHAT'S ON

February/March *Carnival celebrations:* Parades, parties and fancy dress.
March *Moda Lisboa*: Lisbon's most important fashion event.
March/April *Calvary Procession*: Through the Graça district on Good Friday. Easter celebrations throughout the city.
April *Carnation Revolution*: Celebrations to commemorate 25 April 1974.
Bullfighting season: Starts at Campo Pequeno, and continues until October.
Indie Lisboa: International film festival (mid-April).
May *Pilgrimage*: The first annual pilgrimage to Fátima (13 May).
May/June *Rock in Lisboa*: Running over two weekends and attracting big international bands.
June *Major feast days*: 13 June (St. Anthony); 24 June (St. John); 29 June (St. Peter). *The Festas dos Santos* (Festivals of the Saints) take place on and around these three days.
Sintra Festival: Classical music and dance in Sintra's churches and palaces (June and July).
Flea Market: At Sintra (29 June).
August *International Summer Jazz Festival*: Organized by the Calouste Gulbenkian Foundation.
September *Opera Season*: Starts at the Teatro Nacional de São Carlos and runs to June.
October *Pilgrimage*: The second annual pilgrimage to Fátima (mid-October).
December *Lisbon Marathon*: Attracts around 3,500 runners who start and finish at the Praça do Comércio.

Lisbon Online

www.carris.pt
Carries full details of the tram and bus routes run by Carris, the company responsible for most public transport within the city. Also has pages about its various city sightseeing tours.

www.metrolisboa.pt
An excellent site (with English section), with all you need to know about routes, tickets and more on the Lisbon metro system.

www.ana.pt
Portugal's official airport website, with good information on all aspects of the city's Portela Airport, plus other useful tourist information.

www.visitportugal.com
The official site of the Portuguese trade and tourism organization, with tourist information on the country as a whole, including Lisbon.

www.askmelisboa.com
Official tourism site listing information offices and details of the Lisboa Card, which gives free access to transport and most museums.

www.ccb.pt
The site of the Cultural Centre of Belém provides information on forthcoming concerts, exhibitions and other events, as well as highlighting other aspects of the facility's work.

www.portaldasnacoes.pt
An all-embracing site for the attractions, events and activities at the vast Parque das Nações, the former Expo 98 site.

www.ipmuseus.pt
An official site that covers most of Portugal's museums, with links to individual galleries.

www.dn.pt
Useful listings on the website of the *Diario de Notícias*, the Lisbon-based daily newspaper.

GOOD TRAVEL SITES

www.atl-turismolisboa.pt
www.visitlisboa.com
The official site of the Lisbon tourist office, with comprehensive details of hotels, restaurants, transport, museums and other attractions (in English).

www.fodors.com
A travel-planning site. You can research prices and weather; book tickets, cars and rooms, and ask fellow visitors questions. Links to other sites.

INTERNET CAFÉS

Pronto Net
Part of the tourist office. Quick and convenient, but more expensive than most of the city's cybercafés.
K8 Lisbon Welcome Centre, Praça do Comércio 210 312 810 Daily 9–8 €1 for 15 min

Cyberbica
www.cyberbica.com
In the Chiado district south of the Teatro Nacional de São Carlos.
J8 Rua dos Duques de Bragança 7 213 225 004 Mon–Fri 11am–midnight €0.75 for 15 min

Getting There

ENTRY REQUIREMENTS

For the latest passport and visa information, check the British embassy website at www.fco.gov.uk or the United States embassy at www.portugal.usembassy.gov

TOURIST INFORMATION

- Main offices:

Lisboa Welcome Center Praça do Comércio ☎ 210 312 810 🕒 Daily 9–8
Palácio Foz ✉ Praça dos Restauradores ☎ 213 463 314 🕒 Daily 9–8

- There are other offices or kiosks at **Artesanto do Tejo** ✉ Rua do Arsenal 25 ☎ 210 312 820 🕒 Daily 10–6

Santa Apolónia railway station ☎ 218 821 606 🕒 Summer Mon–Sat 9–8, winter Wed–Sat 8–1
Bélem ✉ Mosteiro dos Jerónimos ☎ 213 658 435 🕒 Summer daily 9–7, winter Tue–Sat 10–1, 2–6
Rua Augusta ☎ 213 259 131 🕒 Summer daily 9–7, winter daily 10–1, 2–6
Portela Airport ☎ 218 450 660 🕒 Daily 7am–midnight

AIRPORTS

Internal and international flights use Lisbon's Portela Airport, 7km (4 miles) north of the city. The arrivals hall has a tourist information office, car-rental desks and restaurants. Left luggage is available on the ground level of the P2 car park (north end of arrivals hall).

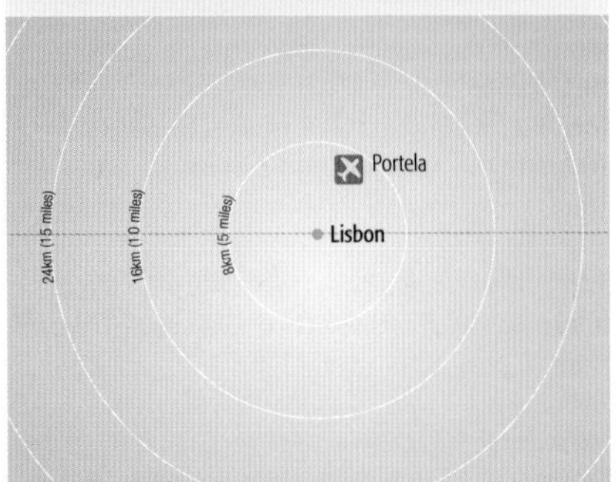

FROM PORTELA AIRPORT

For general airport information ☎ 218 413 500; www.ana.pt.

For flight information consult website or call ☎ 218 413 700.

The Aerobus (www.carris.pt) leaves from outside Arrivals every 20 minutes (🕒 Daily 7.40am–8.15pm), making stops in and around the city. Journey time is around 20–40 minutes. Tickets (from the driver) cost €3.35 and are also valid for a day's travel on the Carris public transport network. Regular city buses (Nos. 5, 22, 44, 45 and 83) leave from outside the airport for various areas of the city, and cost about €1.40.

Taxis operate around the clock from outside the terminal. A ride to the heart of the city should cost €15–€20 (plus €1.50 for luggage and supplements after 10pm and weekends and public holidays). Beware, airport taxis are notorious for overcharging; check that the meter is running or fix a price first, or better still, buy a prepaid taxi voucher from the tourist office in the arrivals hall. Most well-known car-rental companies have desks in the arrivals hall.

ARRIVING BY BUS

International and main regional bus services arrive at the Terminal Rodoviario at Sete Rios, right next to the Jardim Zoológico metro station and just north of the Sete Rios train station. The main national long-distance operator is Rede Expressos (www.rede-expressos.pt), with services from Porto, Faro and other destinations, plus Seville in Spain. International bus services include a daily Eurolines service (☎ 08717 818181 (UK number); www.eurolines.co.uk) from London via Paris. Journey time is 42 hours.

ARRIVING BY CAR

If you are driving to Lisbon, all routes run through Spain. The best and safest option is the E-4 Euro-route, which runs from Madrid via Badajoz. Once in Portugal, it becomes the A6/A2 and heads through the Alentejo to Palmela, where you can choose to continue on the A2 to reach Lisbon via the Ponte 25 de Abril to the city's west, or take the A12 and cross the Tejo on the Ponte Vasco da Gama to the east. The quickest way by car to Lisbon from the UK is by ferry to Bilbao (29–35 hours) or Santander (24 hours). The drive from Santander to Lisbon via Spain and northern Portugal is about 1,000km (620 miles).

ARRIVING BY TRAIN

International trains and services from Porto, Coimbra and other northern towns, plus northern and western suburban services, arrive at Santa Apolónia (☎ 808 208 208). Alternatively you can get off at the Gare do Oriente station at the Parque das Nações and connect with the metro. Trains from the Algarve and elsewhere in the south arrive at Oriente or you can get off at Entrecampos, which is more central, and connect with the metro. Cais do Sodré has services to and from Estoril and Cascais; Rossio or Sete Rios have trains to Sintra, Mafra and other suburban and west-coast destinations. Caminhos de Ferro Portugueses is the national rail company (☎ 808 208 208; www.cp.pt).

INSURANCE

Check your insurance policy and buy any necessary supplements. EU nationals receive reduced cost emergency medical treatment with the relevant documentation (EHIC card for Britons), but full travel insurance is still advised and is vital for all other visitors.

CUSTOMS

Provided it is for personal use, EU nationals can bring back as much as they like, although the following guidelines should be adhered to: 800 cigarettes, 400 cigarillos, 200 cigars, 1kg tobacco; 10 litres of spirits, 20 litres of fortified wine, 90 litres of wine, 110 litres of beer.

CAR RENTAL

All the major car-rental firms have outlets at the airport and in the city. To contact a reputable firm call:

Avis
☎ 218 435 550
www.avis.com
Budget
☎ 210 323 605
www.budget.com
Europcar
☎ 218 401 176
www.europcar.com
Hertz
☎ 218 438 660
www.hertz.com

Getting Around

TOURIST CARD

The highly recommended Lisbon Tourist Card (*Lisboa Card*) gives free admittance to virtually all city museums and other attractions, and unlimited use of public transport. There is also a 65 per cent discount on the Aerobus airport shuttle. It is valid for 24, 48 or 72 hours (€15/€26/€32), and is sold at many outlets, including the tourist offices listed on page 116. Children pay a reduced price. Prepaid taxi vouchers and a 24- and 72-hour Shopping Card (▷ 10) and 72-hour Restaurant Card are also available from the tourist offices. The last two provide discounts at a limited number of selected shops and restaurants.

LOST PROPERTY

Police
First port of call should be the Tourist Police (▷ panel, 121), who have an office open 24 hours.

Metro
✉ Marquês do Pombal Metro, North atrium or Terreiro do Paço
🕓 Mon–Fri 8.30–7.30
☎ 213 500 115

BUSES, TRAMS AND ELEVATORS

Most buses, trams (*eléctricos*) and lifts (*elevadores*) in Lisbon are run by Carris (☎ 213 613 000; www.carris.pt)—yellow booths around the city provide maps, tickets and information. Buy tickets (interchangeable between buses, trams and lifts) from drivers or kiosks; a pass is the best value (▷ 119). The Elevador de Santa Justa runs from Rua Áurea (Rua do Ouro) in the Baixa to Largo do Carmo in the Bairro Alto; the Elevador da Glória funicular runs from Praça dos Restauradores to Rua São Pedro de Alcântara in the Bairro Alto; and the Elevador da Bica goes from Rua de São Paulo to Largo Calhariz-Rua do Loreto. Tickets can be bought from machines (not from the driver) on the new large trams (notably the No. 15). You must have the right coins. Tickets must be validated the first time you use them in the machines on board.

DRIVING IN LISBON

Traffic jams, car theft and a lack of parking make having a car in Lisbon a headache. If you do drive, use a meter or official parking lot. Improperly parked cars are towed away—the local PSP Police station will have details of the nearest pound. Holders of old UK pre-EU green licences should carry an International Driving Permit (IDP). US licences are accepted.

GUIDED TOURS

Trams are an inexpensive way of seeing the city. Tram 28 runs from the Church of São Vicente in the east to the Jardim da Estrela in the west, via the Baixa. Other good routes include the No. 12 from São Tomé to Largo Martim Moniz and the Nos. 15 or 18 (not Sunday) along the waterfront from Praça do Comércio through Belém to Algés. There are two tourist tram routes available: Circuito Colinas and Circuito Descobrimentos; and two open-top bus routes: Circuito Tejo and and Circuito Olisipo—ask at the tourist office. Several companies run trips on the River Tejo (April to October). For shorter trips, go to the quays on the Praça do Comércio

(▷ 26). For two-hour cruises (Mar–Oct) contact Cruzeiros no Tejo (☎ 808 203 050 or 218 824 671; www.transtejo.pt).

METRO

Lisbon also has an efficient four-line Metropolitano (☎ 213 500 115; www.metrolisboa.pt) that runs from 6.30am to 1am. Buy tickets from booths or at machines at the entrance to stations (*estação*). Tickets cost €0.80 per journey in 1 zone, €1.10 per journey in all zones; or €7.51 for a discounted 10-ticket *caderneta* (1 zone, €11.48 for all zones). You can also buy a one-day *Cartão 7 Colinas* (▷ below). Validate the pass on your first journey.

STUDENTS AND SENIOR CITIZENS

Certain museums give discounts to students and senior citizens. Discounted coach and rail travel are available on production of an under-26 youth card.

TAXIS

Lisbon's cream- or black-and-green taxis are cheap and can be hailed on the street (a green light means a cab is free) or picked up from ranks such as those at the Baixa-Chiado metro station or Largo do Camões. Taxi stands are on the Rossio, Praça da Figueira and elsewhere; or phone ☎ 218 119 000 (Radio Taxis), 217 932 756 (Autocoope) or 218 111 100 (Teletaxis). Fares are 20 per cent higher between 9pm and 6am, at weekends and during public holidays.

TRAVEL PASSES

- *Cartão 7 Colinas*: travel passes valid for 1 day (€3.70) for buses, trams, elevators and the metro. This *7 Colinas* card can then be charged with combination tickets and used at will.
- *Bilhete de Bordo*: single-journey tickets (€1.40) available on board and only valid in one zone for buses, trams and elevators.
- Lisboa Card: €15 (1 day), €26 (2 day), €32 (3 day) gives free unlimited travel and free entry to most museums and monuments.

FERRIES

Ferries across the Tejo leave from various points throughout the day. Cais do Sodré river station links Lisbon with Cacilhas. There's also a service from Parque das Nações to Cacilhas, and from Belém to Trafaria. Buy your tickets at the ferry point; a single costs between €0.74 and €2.20, depending on the journey.

VISITORS WITH DISABILITIES

Lisbon's busy, narrow and often steep streets can be difficult for visitors with disabilities. Most public buildings and some museums have ramps and other special access. Obtain the Accessible Tourism Guide from the Secretariado Nacional de Reabilitação (✉ Avenida Conde Valbom 63 ☎ 217 929 500; www.snripd.pt) for details.

WALKING

The best way to discover Lisbon's treasures is definitely on foot. Lisbon Walker operates daily, year-round and offers a range of guided tours around the city. Contact them at their Praça do Comércio meeting point or check the website for details.
✉ Rua dos Remédios 84 (office) ☎ 218 861 840; www.lisbonwalker.com

Essential Facts

ETIQUETTE

Do not wear shorts, miniskirts or skimpy tops in churches, and do not intrude during services. Do not eat or drink in churches. Many churches forbid the use of camera flash and some ban photography. Always be respectful, especially toward people in authority. Smoking is banned in public areas, including public transport.

MONEY

The euro (€) is the official currency of Portugal. Notes come in denominations of 5, 10, 20, 50, 100, 200 and 500 euros, and coins in denominations of 1, 2, 5, 10, 20 and 50 cents, and 1 and 2 euros.

10 euros

50 euros

200 euros

500 euros

ELECTRICITY

- Current is 220 volts AC (50 cycles), but is suitable for 240 volt appliances. Plugs are of the two-round-pin variety.

EMBASSIES

- Canada ✉ Avenida da Liberdade 198–200, 3rd floor ☎ 213 164 600 🕐 Mon–Fri 8.30–12.30, 1.30–5 Ⓜ Avenida
- United Kingdom ✉ Rua de São Bernardo 33 ☎ 213 924 000 🕐 Mon–Fri 9–1, 2.30–5.30 🚌 706, 727; tram 28 Ⓜ Rato
- United States ✉ Avenida das Forças Armadas ☎ 217 273 300 🕐 Mon–Fri 8–5 Ⓜ Entrecampos

MEDICAL AND DENTAL TREATMENT

- Ask your hotel for details of local doctors or call the British Hospital for advice (▷ below).
- British Hospital: Most staff here speak English, but there is no emergency department ✉ Rua Saraiva de Carvalho 49 ☎ 213 943 100 🚌 9; tram 25, 28. For emergencies head to CUF Descobertas ✉ Parque das Nações ☎ 210 025 200 (Private so insurance needed).
- Details of pharmacies' 24-hour rota services are posted on pharmacy doors and in local newspapers. Normal opening is Mon–Fri 9–1, 3–7, Sat 9–1.

MONEY MATTERS

- Foreign exchange bureaux (*cambios*) and banks with exchange facilities are generally open Mon–Fri 8.30–3. You can also change money at the airport and Santa Apolónia railway station (24-hour services), the main post office and automatic exchange machines. Automatic Teller Machines (ATMs), or Multibanco, give credit card cash advances.
- Commission rates on travellers' cheques are often high. Savings banks or building societies (*caixas*) may charge cheaper rates.
- Credit cards are widely accepted, though it is best to have cash on hand as some bars and shops do not take cards.

OPENING TIMES

- Shops: Traditional shops: Mon–Fri 10–1, 3–7; Sat 10–1. Chain stores: Mon–Sat 10–7. Malls: Daily 10–midnight.
- Museums: 10–1, 2–6. Important museums may remain open all day but times vary. Most are closed on Monday.
- Churches: 10–6. Some open only for early morning and evening services.

PUBLIC HOLIDAYS

- 1 Jan: New Year's Day; Feb/Mar Shrove Tuesday; Good Friday/Easter Monday; 25 Apr: Liberation Day; 1 May: May Day; Corpus Christi (late May or early Jun); 10 Jun: Camões Day; 13 Jun: St. Anthony's Day; 15 Aug: Assumption; 5 Oct: Republic Day; 1 Nov: All Saints' Day; 1 Dec: Independence Day; 8 Dec: Immaculate Conception; 25 Dec: Christmas Day

SENSIBLE PRECAUTIONS

- Don't carry large amounts of cash; use credit cards or travellers' cheques.
- Be on your guard against pickpockets on crowded buses, in markets and streets, and beware of strap-cutting thieves.
- Avoid the port, railway station, parks and the Alfama after dark.

TELEPHONES

- The Lisbon area code is 21 and must be dialled regardless of where you call from. It is followed by a seven-digit number. Numbers in this guide are given inclusive of this area code.
- Telecom pay phones are found in bars, cafés, tourist offices, newsagents and on street corners.
- Public phones accept all euro coins, and increasingly accept credit cards or phone cards available from post offices, kiosks and shops displaying the PT (Portugal Telecom) logo.
- English-speaking operator for reverse charge (collect) calls abroad, or dialling problems 171 (Europe and intercontinental). Information on international calls 179 National Directory 118

POSTAL SERVICES

- Post offices are *correios*. Letter boxes are red.
- Lisbon's main post office (*Correio Geral*) is at Praça do Comércio 213 220 920 Mon–Fri 8.30–6.30.
- There is another large office on Praça dos Restauradores Mon–Fri 8–10, Sat, Sun 9–6
- Other post offices usually open Mon–Fri 8 or 9–6. Smaller offices may open 8 or 9–12.30 and 2.30–6. Main offices may open on Saturday morning.
- Buy stamps (*selos*) at post offices or shops displaying the sign 'CTT Selos' or 'Correio de Portugal Selos'.
- Current prices for postcards and letters are €0.67 (EU) and €0.80 (other foreign destinations).
- Airmail is *por avião*. The quickest express service is *Correio Azul*.

EMERGENCIES

Police, Fire or Ambulance 112

For general enquiries and to report a crime or theft, the Tourist Police have an office open 24 hours a day:

Palácio Foz, Praça dos Restauradores

213 421 634

Language

Portuguese is a Romance language, so a knowledge of French, Spanish or Italian will help you decipher the written word. The spoken word is a different thing. The pronunciation is difficult, at least at the outset.

USEFUL WORDS AND PHRASES	
yes/no	*sim/não*
please	*por favor*
thank you	*obrigado (said by a man), obrigada (said by a woman)*
hello	*olá*
goodbye	*adeus*
good morning	*bom dia*
good afternoon	*boa tarde*
goodnight	*boa noite*
excuse me	*com licença*
I'm sorry	*desculpe*
how much?	*quanto?*
where	*onde*
big/little	*grande/pequeno*
inexpensive	*barato*
expensive	*caro*
today	*hoje*
tomorrow	*amanhã*
yesterday	*ontem*
open/closed	*aberto/fechado*
men	*homens*
women	*senhoras*
I don't understand	*não compreendo*
how much is it?	*quanto custa?*
at what time...?	*a que horas...?*
please help me	*ajude-me por favor*
do you speak English?	*fala inglês?*
How are you?	*Como está?*
Fine, thank you	*Bem obrigado/a*
My name is...	*chamo-me...*
sorry	*desculpe/perdão*

RESTAURANT	
alcohol	*alcool*
beer	*cerveja*
bill	*conta*
bread	*pão*
café	*café*
coffee	*café*
dinner	*jantar*
lunch	*almoço*
menu	*menú/ementa*
milk	*leite*
pepper	*pimenta*
salt	*sal*
table	*mesa*
tea	*chá*
waiter	*empregado/a*

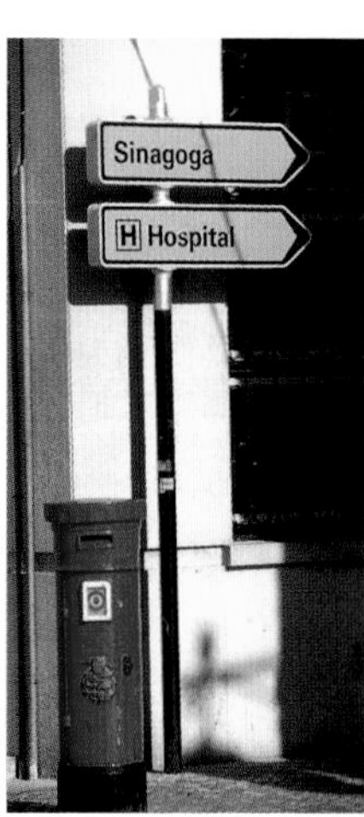

TOURING	
airport	*aeroporto*
boat	*barco*
bus station	*estação de camionetas*
coach	*autocarro*
car	*automóvel*
square	*praça*
street	*rua*
taxi rank	*praça de táxis*
train	*comboio*
station	*estação*

EMERGENCY	
help	*socorro*
stop	*pare*
stop that thief	*apanhe o ladrão*
police	*polícia*
fire	*fogo*
leave me alone	*deixe-me em paz*
I've lost my purse/wallet	*Perdi o meu porta-moedas/a minha carteira*
Could you call a doctor quickly?	*podia chamar um médico depressa?*
hospital	*hospital*

ACCOMMODATION	
does that include breakfast?	*Está incluido o pequeno almoço?*
balcony	*varanda*
air-conditioning	*ar condicionado*
bathroom	*casa de banho*
chambermaid	*camareira*
hot water	*água quente*
key	*chave*
lift	*elevador*
room	*quarto*
room service	*serviço de quarto*
shower	*duche*
telephone	*telefone*
towel	*toalha*
water	*água*

NUMBERS	
0	*zero*
1	*um*
2	*dois*
3	*três*
4	*quatro*
5	*cinco*
6	*seis*
7	*sete*
8	*oito*
9	*nove*
10	*dez*
11	*onze*
12	*doze*
13	*treze*
14	*catorze*
15	*quinze*
16	*dezasseis*
17	*dezassete*
18	*dezoito*
19	*dezanove*
20	*vinte*
100	*cem*
500	*quinhentos*

DAYS OF THE WEEK	
Sunday	*Domingo*
Monday	*Segunda-feira*
Tuesday	*Terça-feira*
Wednesday	*Quarta-feira*
Thursday	*Quinta-feira*
Friday	*Sexta-feira*
Saturday	*Sábado*

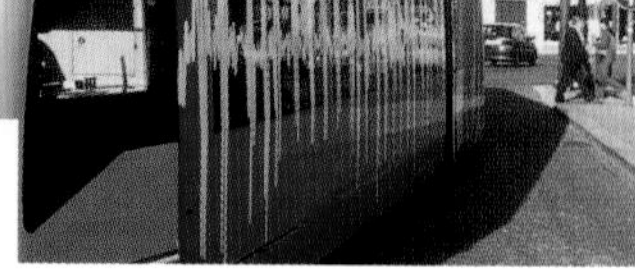

Timeline

EARTHQUAKE

The Great Earthquake of 1755 began at 9.30am on 1 November—All Saints Day—when many people were at church. The effects of three tremors in 10 minutes were made far worse by a tidal wave, 12.5m (41ft) high, and by fires as countless church candles were thrown over. Shock waves were felt as far away as Scotland and Jamaica. An estimated 60,000 people were killed in Lisbon. Corpses were sunk out at sea to halt epidemics. Taxes were suspended and prices fixed by emergency decree. Around 9,000 buildings were destroyed, but the Marquês de Pombal masterminded the reconstruction of the city.

711 The Moors take control of much of Portugal, including Lisbon.

1139 Afonso Henriques, son of a French count and Castilian princess, declares himself first king of 'Portucale'.

1147 Afonso captures Lisbon from the Moors with soldiers bound for the Second Crusade.

1249 The loss of Faro marks the end of Moorish power in Portugal.

1255 King Afonso III makes Lisbon capital of Portugal, in place of Coimbra.

1385 The Portuguese victory against Castile at the Battle of Aljubarrota secures Portuguese independence for some 200 years.

1580 A crisis in the Portuguese succession allows Philip II of Spain to invade.

1640 Spanish are overthrown and replaced by the Bragança dynasty of Portuguese kings.

1755 The Great Earthquake destroys two-thirds of Lisbon (▷ panel).

1807 Portugal refuses to join Napoleon's naval blockade of Britain, its ally, and is attacked by a French army.

1810 During the ensuing Peninsular Wars, the Duke of Wellington builds fortifications known as

A statue of Afonso Henriques, the first king of Portugal (below left); mosaic on the Arco de Repouso in Faro (below middle); ruins of Lisbon's cathedral after the earthquake of 1755 (below right)

the Lines of Torres Vedras to protect Lisbon.

1834 The end of the 'War of the Two Brothers' between Dom Pedro IV, emperor of Brazil, and Dom Miguel.

1908 King Carlos I is assassinated.

1910 The Portuguese monarchy is overthrown and replaced by a republic.

1932 Dr. António de Oliveira Salazar is made Prime Minister and rules as a dictator until 1968.

1974 The Carnation Revolution of 25 April ends some 40 years of dictatorship.

1986 Portugal joins the European Community (now the European Union).

2002 Euro notes and coins come into circulation, replacing the escudo.

2004 Portugal hosts Euro 2004, the European football championship.

2007 The European Crime and Safety Survey reveals Lisbon as one of the top three safest capitals in Europe.

2009 Portuguese soccer continues to make history as Cristiano Ronaldo is named FIFA player of the year and is transferred to Real Madrid for a record €80 million fee.

SEEKING NEW LANDS

In 1419 Henry the Navigator's first square-rigged *barcas* set out in search of a sea route to the Orient. The ship reached Madeira and, eight years later, the Azores.
In 1498 four ships under Vasco da Gama left Lisbon and pioneered a sea route to the East Indies, thus breaking the monopoly of Venetian and Ottoman traders in the East. Two years later, in 1500, Pedro Álvares Cabral 'discovered' Brazil, whose riches helped to make Portugal the wealthiest country in Europe.

Exhibits in the Museu Militar bear witness to the battles fought in Portugal's turbulent past (below left); Philip II of Spain (below middle); Torre de Belém was built as a lookout post between 1515 and 1520 (below right)

Index

A
accommodation 108–112
air travel 116
Alfama 8, 42–43, 52
antiques 11, 12, 32, 34, 53
architecture, contemporary 5
ATMs 120
Avenida da Liberdade 30

B
Bairro Alto 8, 58
Bairro Alto/the West 55–72
  entertainment and nightlife 67–68
  map 56–57
  restaurants 69–72
  shopping 66
  sights 58–64
  tour 65
Baixa 8, 24
Baixa-Chiado 20–38
  entertainment and nightlife 36
  map 22–23
  restaurants 36–38
  shopping 28–29, 32–35
  sights 24–30
  walk 31
banks 120
Barcelos Cock 66
Basílica da Estrela 9, 59
Belém 83–96
  map 84–85
  restaurants 96
  sights 86–95
bookshops 12, 33, 34, 66
budget travellers 16, 109
bullfighting 114
buses
  city buses 118
  long-distance 117

C
cable car 103
Camões, Luíz de 91
Campo de Santa Clara 9, 44
car rental 117
Castelo de São Jorge 9, 46–47
cathedral (Sé) 8, 48–49
Centro de Arte Moderna 9, 80
Centro Cultural de Belém 94
Chiado 8, 28–29, 31
children's entertainment 18
Christ, statue of 65
church opening hours 121
churches
  Basílica da Estrela 9, 59
  Igreja da Madre de Deus 9, 100–101
  Igreja dos Mártires 29
  Igreja de São Roque 9, 60–61
  Nossa Senhora da Conceiçao Velha 50
  Santa Engrácia 50–51
  Santa Luzia 51
  Santo António de Lisboa 51
  São Vicente de Fora 51
  Sé 8, 48–49
cinemas 36
City Museum 104
classical music venues 36
climate and seasons 114
clubs 13, 18, 53, 67–68
concessions 118, 119
credit cards 120
crime 121
customs regulations 117
cybercafés 115

D
Decorative Arts Museum 9, 45
dental treatment 120
disabilities, visitors with 119
Dom Pedro IV statue 27
driving 117, 118

E
earthquake (1755) 124
eating out 14–15
  bills 96
  eating times 14
  half portions 54
  Portuguese cuisine 14, 15, 16
  tipping 96
  see also restaurants
electricity 120
Elevador da Bica 118
Elevador da Glória 58, 118
Elevador de Santa Justa 30, 118
embassies 120
embroideries 32, 35
emergencies 121
entertainment and nightlife 13
  Bairro Alto/the West 67–68
  Baixa-Chiado 36
  Mouraria–Alfama 53
etiquette 120
excursions 106
  Mafra 106
  Sintra 106

F
fado 18, 50, 53, 58, 67, 68
Fado Museum 50
fashion shopping 12, 32, 35, 66
ferries 65, 118–119
festivals and events 114
flea market 11, 44
food shopping 11, 12, 34, 53, 66
foreign exchange 120
funiculars 30, 58

G
Gama, Vasco da 86, 87, 125
gardens and parks
  Jardim Botânico 64
  Jardim Boto Machado 44
  Jardim Guerra Junqueiro 64
  Palácio dos Marqueses de Fronteira 78–79
  Parque Eduardo VII 81
  Parque Florestal de Monsanto 81
  Parque das Nações 5, 8, 103
gay scene 67, 68
gifts and souvenirs 11, 12, 17
Gulbenkian Museum 9, 76–77

H
handicrafts 12, 32, 33, 35
Henry the Navigator 91, 125
history 124–125
hotels 16, 108, 109–112

I
Igreja da Madre de Deus 9, 100–101
Igreja dos Mártires 29
Igreja de São Roque 9, 60–61
insurance 117

J
Jardim Botânico 64
Jardim Boto Machado 44
Jardim Guerra Junqueiro 64
Jardim Zoológico de Lisboa 81
jewellery 12, 34, 35
José I statue 26

L
language 122–123
Lisboa Card 10, 118, 119
Lisbon environs 97–106
  excursions 106
  map 98–99
  sights 100–105
lost property 118

M
Mafra 106
Maritime Museum 9, 88–89
markets 11, 44, 53, 66
medical treatment 120

menu reader 71
Metro 119
Military Museum 50
Miradoura de São Pedro de Alcântara 64
Modern Art, Centre for 9, 80
money 120
Monument to the Discoveries 8, 91
Mosteiro dos Jerónimos 9, 86–87
Mouraria–Alfama 39–54
entertainment and nightlife 53
map 40–41
restaurants 54
shopping 53
sights 42–51
walk 52
museum opening hours 121
museums and galleries
Centro de Arte Moderna 9, 80
Museu Arqueológico do Carmo 9, 25
Museu das Artes Decorativas 9, 45
Museu Calouste Gulbenkian 9, 76–77
Museu e Casa do Fado 50
Museu do Chiado 30
Museu da Cidade 104
Museu Etnológico da Sociedade de Geografia 30
Museu de Marinha 9, 88–89
Museu da Marioneta 64
Museu da Música 104
Museu Nacional de Arqueólogia 94
Museu Nacional de Arte Antiga 9, 62–63
Museu Nacional do Azulejo 9, 102
Museu Nacional dos Coches 8, 90
Museu Nacional Militar 50
Museu Nacional do Teatro 104
Museu Nacional do Traje 104–105
Museu Presidéncia da República 94
Music Museum 104
music, traditional 18

N
National Archaeological Museum 94
National Coach Museum 8, 90
National Museum of Ancient Art 9, 62–63
National Museum of Costume 104–105
National Theatre Museum 104
National Tile Museum 9, 102
Nossa Senhora da Conceiçao Velha 50

O
Oceanário 105
opening times 121
opera 36

P
Padrão dos Descobrimentos 8, 91
Palácio dos Marqueses de Fronteira 8, 78–79
Parque Eduardo VII 81
Parque Florestal de Monsanto 81
Parque das Nações 5, 8, 103
passports and visas 116
pastelarias 15, 37
Pavilhão do Conhecimento–Ciência Viva 105
pensões 108
personal safety 121
pharmacies 120
Planetário Calouste Gulbenkian 94
Planetarium 94
police 121
Pombal, Marquês de 24, 27
population 4
port 33, 34, 72
post offices 121
postal services 121
Praça do Comércio 8, 26
Praça Dom Pedro IV *see* Rossio
public holidays 121
public transport 118–119
Puppet Museum 64

R
residenciais 108
restaurants 15, 16
Bairro Alto/the West 69–72
Baixa-Chiado 36–38
Belém 96
Mouraria–Alfama 54
river trips 118–119
Rossio 8, 27

S
salt cod 16
Santa Engrácia 50–51
Santa Luzia 51
Santo António de Lisboa 51
São Sebastião 73–82
map 74–75
sights 76–82
São Vicente de Fora 51
sardines 14
Sé 8, 48–49
senior citizens 119
shopping 10–12
Bairro Alto/the West 66
Baixa–Chiado 28–29, 32–35
Lisboa Shopping Card 10, 118
malls 11
markets 11, 44, 53, 66
Mouraria–Alfama 53
opening times 121
Sintra 106
smoking etiquette 120
Solar do Vinho do Porto 58
student visitors 119

T
tascas 38
taxis 116, 119
Tejo (Tagus) 65
Teleférico 103
telephones 121
theatre 36
tiles (*azulejos*) 5, 11, 12, 17, 33, 34, 53, 79, 102
time differences 114
tipping 96
Torre de Belém 8, 92–93
Torre Vasco da Gama 103
tourist information 115, 116
tours, guided 118–119
train services 117
trams 4, 118
travel passes 119
travellers' cheques 120
two-day itinerary 6–7

W
walks
Across the Tejo 65
Alfama 52
Chiado 31
websites 115
wines 33–34, 53

Z
zoo 81

Lisbon's
25 Best

WRITTEN BY Tim Jepson
ADDITIONAL WRITING Hilary Weston and Jackie Staddon
UPDATED BY Emma Rowley Ruas
DESIGN WORK Jacqueline Bailey
COVER DESIGN Tigist Getachew
INDEXER Marie Lorimer
IMAGE RETOUCHING AND REPRO Sarah Montgomery and James Tims
PROJECT EDITOR Kim Lehoucka
REVIEWING EDITOR Laura Kidder
SERIES EDITOR Marie-Claire Jefferies

© AA Media Limited 2010 (registered office: Fanum House, Basing View, Basingstoke, Hampshire RG21 4EA, registered number 06112600).

All rights reserved. Published in the United States by Fodor's Travel, a division of Random House, Inc., and simultaneously in Canada by Random House of Canada Limited, Toronto. Distributed by Random House, Inc., New York. No maps, illustrations, or other portions of this book may be reproduced in any form without written permission from the publishers.

Fodor's is a registered trademark of Random House, Inc.
Published in the United Kingdom by AA Publishing

ISBN 978-1-4000-0393-8

FOURTH EDITION

IMPORTANT TIP
Time inevitably brings changes, so always confirm prices, travel facts, and other perishable information when it matters. Although Fodor's cannot accept responsibility for errors, you can use this guide in the confidence that we have taken every care to ensure its accuracy.

SPECIAL SALES
This book is available for special discounts for bulk purchases for sales promotions or premiums. Special editions, including personalized covers, excerpts of existing books, and corporate imprints, can be created in large quantities for special needs. For more information, write to Special Markets/Premium Sales, 1745 Broadway, MD 6–2, New York, NY 10019 or email specialmarkets@randomhouse.com.

Color separation by Keenes, Andover, UK
Printed and bound by Leo Paper Products, China
10 9 8 7 6 5 4 3 2 1

A04019
Maps in this title produced from mapping © MAIRDUMONT / Falk Verlag 2010
Transport map © Communicarta Ltd, UK

The Automobile Association wishes to thank the following photographers, companies and picture libraries for their assistance in the preparation of this book.

Abbreviations for the picture credits are as follows – (t) top; (b) bottom; (l) left; (r) right; (c) centre; (AA) AA World Travel Library.

1 AA/A Kouprianoff; **2–18t** AA; **4cl** AA/A Kouprianoff; **5c/b** AA/A Mockford & N Bonetti; **6cl** AA/T Harris; **6cc** AA/T Harris; **6cr** AA/P Wilson; **6bl** AA/A Kouprianoff; **6cc** AA/T Harris; **6cr** AA/A Kouprianoff; **7cl** AA/A Kouprianoff; **7cc** AA/T Harris; **7cr** AA/A Mockford & N Bonetti; **7bl** AA/T Harris; **7bc** AA/T Harris; **7br** AA/P Wilson; **10/11t** AA/M Birkitt; **10cr** AA/A Mockford & N Bonetti; **10/11c** AA/T Harris; **10/11b** AA/A Mockford & N Bonetti; **11cl** AA/A Mockford & N Bonetti; **12b** AA/A Mockford & N Bonetti; **13ctl** AA/A Mockford & N Bonetti; **13cl** AA/A Mockford & N Bonetti; **13bl** AA/A Mockford & N Bonetti; **14tcr** A Kouprianoff; **14cr** A Kouprianoff; **14bcr** A Kouprianoff; **14br** AA/T Harris; **15b** AA/A Mockford & N Bonetti; **16(i)** AA/M Wells; **16(ii)** AA/A Mockford & N Bonetti; **16(iii)** AA/M Wells; **16(iv)** AA/A Kouprianoff; **17(i)** AA/A Kouprianoff; **17(ii)** AA/A Kouprianoff; **17(iii)** AA/A Mockford & N Bonetti; **17(iv)** AA/T Harris; **18(i)** AA/T Harris; **18(ii)** AA/P Wilson; **18(iii)** Digitalvision; **18(iv)** AA/T Harris; **19(i)** AA/A Mockford & N Bonetti; **19(ii)** AA/A Mockford & N Bonetti; **19(iii)** AA/A Mockford & N Bonetti; **19(iv)** Fundação Calouste Gulbenkian; **19(v)** AA/A Kouprianoff; **19(vi)** AA/T Harris; **20/21** AA/A Mockford & N Bonetti; **24l** AA/A Kouprianoff; **24r** AA/A Mockford & N Bonetti; **25l** AA/M Wells; **25r** AA/M Wells; **26l** AA/A Mockford & N Bonetti; **26c** AA/A Mockford & N Bonetti; **26r** AA/A Mockford & N Bonetti; **27l** AA/T Harris; **27c** AA/T Harris; **27r** AA/T Harris; **28** AA/A Kouprianoff; **28/29** AA/A Mockford & N Bonetti; **29** AA/A Mockford & N Bonetti; **30t** AA/T Harris; **30bl** AA/M Wells; **30br** AA/A Kouprianoff; **31t** AA/A Kouprianoff; **32–35t** AA/A Mockford & N Bonetti; **36t** AA/A Mockford & N Bonetti; **36c** AA/A Mockford & N Bonetti; **37–38t** AA/A Mockford & N Bonetti; **39** AA/A Kouprianoff; **42tl** AA/A Kouprianoff; **42tr** AA/A Mockford & N Bonetti; **42/43c** AA/A Mockford & N Bonetti; **43t** AA/A Mockford & N Bonetti; **43cr** AA/T Harris; **44l** AA/A Kouprianoff; **44r** AA/M Birkitt; **45l** AA/A Kouprianoff; **45r** AA/A Kouprianoff; **46tl** AA/M Wells; **46tr** AA/M Wells; **47** AA/M Wells; **48l** AA/M Wells; **48/49** AA/A Mockford & N Bonetti; **50/51t** AA/A Mockford & N Bonetti; **50b** AA/A Kouprianoff; **51b** AA/A Kouprianoff; **52** AA/M Wells; **53t** AA/A Mockford & N Bonetti; **53c** AA/A Mockford & N Bonetti; **54** AA/A Mockford & N Bonetti; **55** AA/A Mockford & N Bonetti; **58l** AA/A Mockford & N Bonetti; **58r** AA/M Birkitt; **59l** AA/A Kouprianoff; **59c** AA/A Kouprianoff; **59r** AA/A Kouprianoff; **60l** AA/A Kouprianoff; **60/61** AA/A Kouprianoff; **62tl** AA/A Kouprianoff; **62tr** AA/A Kouprianoff; **62cr** AA/A Kouprianoff; **63t** AA/A Kouprianoff; **63cl** AA/A Kouprianoff; **63cr** AA/A Kouprianoff; **64t** AA/A Kouprianoff; **64bl** AA/A Kouprianoff; **64br** AA/A Kouprianoff; **65t** AA/A Kouprianoff; **66t** AA/A Mockford & N Bonetti; **67–68t** AA/P Wilson; **69** AA/P Wilson; **70** AA/M Wells; **71–72** AA/P Wilson; **73** AA/A Kouprianoff; **76tl** Fundação Calouste Gulbenkian; **76tr** Fundação Calouste Gulbenkian; **76cr** Fundação Calouste Gulbenkian; **77t** Fundação Calouste Gulbenkian; **77cl** Fundação Calouste Gulbenkian; **77cr** Fundação Calouste Gulbenkian; **78t** AA/A Kouprianoff; **78c** AA/A Kouprianoff; **79t** AA/A Kouprianoff; **79c** AA/A Kouprianoff; **80l** AA/A Kouprianoff; **80r** Fundação Calouste Gulbenkian; **81t** AA/P Wilson; **81b** AA/M Wells; **82** AA/M Wells; **83** AA/A Kouprianoff; **86l** AA/A Kouprianoff; **86/87t** AA/A Kouprianoff; **86/87c** AA/A Kouprianoff; **87r** AA/A Kouprianoff; **88l** Museu de Marinha; **88/89t** Museu de Marinha; **88/89c** Museu de Marinha; **89tr** Museu de Marinha; **89cr** Museu de Marinha; **90l** AA/A Kouprianoff; **90r** AA/A Kouprianoff; **91l** AA/A Kouprianoff; **91r** AA/A Kouprianoff; **92** AA/A Kouprianoff; **92/93** AA/A Kouprianoff; **93** AA/P Wilson; **94t** AA/A Kouprianoff; **94b** Planetário Calouste Gulbenkian; **95** AA/M Wells; **96** AA/A Mockford & N Bonetti; **97** AA/A Mockford & N Bonetti; **100l** AA/A Kouprianoff; **100/101** AA/A Kouprianoff; **102l** AA/A Kouprianoff; **102r** AA/A Kouprianoff; **103l** AA/T Harris; **103r** AA/A Mockford & N Bonetti; **104–105t** AA/T Harris; **104b** AA/M Wells; **105bl** AA/M Wells; **105br** AA/M Wells; **106** AA/T Harris; **107** AA/C Sawyer; **108–112t** AA/C Sawyer; **108tcr** AA/C Sawyer; **108cr** AA/D Henley; **108bcr** AA/A Mockford & N Bonetti; **108br** AA/J Smith; **113** AA/A Mockford & N Bonetti; **114–125t** AA/A Mockford & N Bonetti; **120** European Central Bank; **122** AA/T Harris; **124bl** AA/A Kouprianoff; **124bc** AA/C Jones; **124br** AA; **125bl** AA/A Kouprianoff; **125cb** AA; **125br** AA/P Wilson

Every effort has been made to trace the copyright holders, and we apologise in advance for any accidental errors. We would be pleased to apply any corrections in any following edition of this publication.